DEVOTE

40

DAYS

DEVOTE

40

DAYS

JANE JAYROE
&
FAITH-FILLED FRIENDS

TATE PUBLISHING & *Enterprises*

Scriptures marked as (CEV) are taken from the Contemporary English Version, Copyright © 1995 by American Bible Society. Used by permission.

Scripture quotations marked (KJV) are taken from the *Holy Bible, King James Version,* Cambridge, 1769. Used by permission. All rights reserved.

Scripture quotations marked (NASB) are taken from the New American Standard Bible®, Copyright © 1960, 1962, 1963, 1968, 1971, 1972, 1973, 1975, 1977, 1995 by The Lockman Foundation. Used by permission.

Scripture quotations marked (NKJV) are taken from the New King James Version®. Copyright © 1982 by Thomas Nelson, Inc. Used by permission. All rights reserved.

Scripture quotations marked (NIV) are taken from the *Holy Bible, New International Version®.* NIV®. Copyright© 1973, 1978, 1984 by International Bible Society. Used by permission of Zondervan. All rights reserved.

Scripture quotations marked (NRSV) are from New Revised Standard Version Bible, copyright © 1989 National Council of the Churches of Christ in the United States of America. Used by permission. All rights reserved.

Scripture quotations marked (MSG) are taken from *The Message.* Copyright © 1993, 1994, 1995, 1996, 2000, 2001, 2002. Used by permission of NavPress Publishing Group.

Scripture quotations marked (RSV) are from *Revised Standard Version of the Bible,* copyright © 1946, 1952, and 1971 National Council of the Churches of Christ in the United States of America. Used by permission. All rights reserved.

Scripture quotations marked (GNT) are from the *Good News Translation in Today's English Version-* Second Edition Copyright © 1992 by American Bible Society. Used by Permission.

The opinions expressed by the author are not necessarily those of Tate Publishing, LLC.

Published by Tate Publishing & Enterprises, LLC
127 E. Trade Center Terrace | Mustang, Oklahoma 73064 USA
1.888.361.9473 | www.tatepublishing.com

Tate Publishing is committed to excellence in the publishing industry. The company reflects the philosophy established by the founders, based on Psalm 68:11,
"The Lord gave the word and great was the company of those who published it."

Book design copyright © 2010 by Tate Publishing, LLC. All rights reserved.
Cover design by Rebekah Garibay
Interior design by Stefanie Rane

Published in the United States of America

ISBN: 978-1-61739-098-2
1. Religion, Christian Life, Devotional
2. Religion, Christian Life, Women's Issues
10.12.06

DEDICATION

Dedicated to my husband,
Jerry Gamble,
for his love and support.

ACKNOWLEDGMENTS

Thanks to all the women who have made this book possible. From the encouragement of friends to my faith-sharing group of "Esther Women," to the contributors—you are the energy that shapes my day. Also, gratitude goes out to writing teacher and author extraordinaire, Carolyn Wall, and her group of writers who have included me in a gracious and helpful way.

Karen Waddell, Bobbie Roe, Lori Bedford, and Leann Overstake carefully read the manuscript; and M. J. Alexander contributed her artistic gifts for the cover photograph. I appreciate them. This book contains devotionals written by women who are at the front of many professions and who contribute every day to a better world. I am proud to count them as spiritual sisters.

Thanks to you, the reader. May you find God in the midst of these humble efforts.

TABLE OF CONTENTS

INTRODUCTION

I have always prayed—in the car, on the fly, or in bed at night before I nod off. It's not been much of a concentrated effort. Truthfully, I haven't always been convinced that it made a difference.

If I was facing a crisis, I prayed a lot just in case.

In April of 2000, a speaker at my church spent a Saturday talking about the power of prayer. Her life had been totally transformed by the discipline of prayer and devotional time. I was convinced. From that day forward I made a serious commitment to a dedicated time with God … not just when it fit my schedule, but first thing in the morning before the day crowded in.

I asked myself, "Is prayer a priority, a preference, or another item to fit on my 'to do' list between phone calls, emails, work, meetings, and groceries?" I chose to put the dedicated time at the top of my list for a few months—it's been almost ten years since.

The decision to create this daily sacred space took place during an extremely demanding time in my career; the effort was not insignificant. First, I started praying that God would wake me up earlier in order to have this time. I'm not a morning person. In fact, most of my career was spent co-anchoring television news at ten o'clock in the evening. My work hours had been from two p.m. to eleven p.m. But now my schedule as director of the Oklahoma Department of Tourism demanded arriving at my office early. Arranging for devotional time before I left home was a challenge.

Still, on that day in April, God was calling me, by name, into a deeper relationship—not based on sudden needs or emotional inspiration but a practical disciplined need to grow as a Christian. I wanted to make the spiritual dimension of my life a regular habitat instead of an occasional vacation.

The concept wasn't new. Growing up, I was an athlete—a tournament-winning basketball player. I was also a musician. My mother insisted I take piano lessons, and I wanted voice training. Performing was my passion.

Can you imagine having the endurance to play basketball without putting in the hours of running laps, learning plays, practicing the fundamentals of the game? How many of us can sit down on a piano bench and have our hands magically produce music without years of fingering scales, practicing complicated pieces, and studying music theory?

Even though I'd grown up in a Christian home and attended church my whole life, I knew there was something more. How, then, to move forward? The obvious way was to devote regular time to seek God with nothing else on my agenda.

I set the stage by choosing a place in my home that I could return to daily. It was a chair next to a window upstairs that I could open; I kept my journal, Bible, devotional books, pens, and paper on the hassock in front of me. It became my sacred spot in the house.

In no time, after beginning this new habit, I experienced a difference. To begin the morning feeling centered, positive, loved, and connected was an amazing gift. Sometimes, that good feeling didn't last long before I fluttered into the frenzies of my schedule, but as I've continued through the years, the blessed feeling stretches farther and farther into my day.

Often, the set aside time brought specific answers to problems I had struggled with the night before.

Just like relationships with husbands, parents, children, and friends—connecting spiritually is a lifelong pursuit. It must be nurtured, sustained, and inspired consistently. What would your relationship with your husband be if you never communicated with him? There are couples like that—existing side by side but without a deep, caring bond. It takes focused time together to create the tie that binds. Our souls cry out for the same experience with God.

When we add this habit of daily devotional time, our inner life is transformed and then our behavior. It's not a straight line toward intimacy but rather zigs and zags on the way upward.

Do you feel empty? Discouraged, flustered, afraid, worried, sad, or frustrated? Do you wonder if God has a purpose for you, or maybe you question that life really matters? We all find ourselves floundering at one time or another. Devote forty days to finding some answers.

Why forty? God has used this spiritual timeline throughout the Bible. Moses spent forty days on Mount Sinai; Jesus was in the wilderness for forty days and nights in preparation for His ministry. Forty days was the time between the resurrection of Jesus and His ascension.

We can spend the next few weeks doing the same things and expecting different results, or we can carve out a little time in the morning and change our lives. The choice is ours to make.

When I experience holy moments every morning, the rest of my day goes better. Begin with small increments, maybe five minutes. Soon you'll want much more.

To help with this blessed transition, I have put together this book of devotionals. Most are based on my experiences that I hope will help you. Many of my friends have contributed as well— some of the most influential and busy women I know. Participants include a stay-at-home mom, a State Supreme Court Justice, a busy doctor, a friend with a precious sister, an award winning broadcast journalist, a merchant, a counselor, a banker, a politician, first ladies, teachers, a successful coach, and extraordinary volunteers. They represent many Christian denominations but one voice. They joyfully add their personal stories for the encouragement of other women. Prayerfully, every devotional will bring insight and new blessings to your prayer time.

God calls His beloved children to relationship. Will you join others in choosing to hear His voice? The body of Christ limps without you.

Begin tonight, proclaiming with the Psalmist: *"Let the morning bring word of Your unfailing love, for I have put my trust in You"* (Psalm 143:8).

Devote forty days—for a profound difference.

Jane Jayroe

Jane Jayroe

STRENGTHENED BY STORMS

His way is in the whirlwind and the storm, and clouds are the dust of His feet.

—Nahum 1:3 NIV

Springtime storms were as common as our red dirt when I was growing up in rural Oklahoma. A tornado could swoop down from a black sky and, like a giant lawnmower, tear up a community in minutes. Often in the middle of the night, the threatening clouds caused the town's fire siren to pierce the air. Our safe spot was a cellar across the back alley.

Pulled from a warm bed, I pretended to be asleep so my daddy would carry me. Mother held sister's hand as we rushed out the kitchen door toward the neighbor's shelter. The wind slapped the pink Cinderella nightgown around my skinny legs, and the stringy brown hair on my head blew about like one of those dirt devils that danced in our fields.

I tucked my head into Daddy's neck. His one arm held me up while the other circled Mother's shoulders. All was safe in my world—my daddy was carrying me.

Since those early days I have experienced different kinds of storms: the disturbance of a divorce and the despair that followed, the unrest of loneliness, the downpour of fear, the turmoil of financial anxiety, cancer, insecurity, and the emptiness of loss.

I learned important lessons on my turbulent journey of faith:

1. *The storm passes.*

Measured in minutes or years—tough times don't last forever. We are promised in the

Twenty-third Psalm, that we walk *through* the valley of the shadow of death—we don't set up camp there.

2. *You're not alone.*

When the weather turns bad, there's nothing more comforting than the arms of the Father. In the light of today and with the distance of age, I know that my daddy *was* vulnerable. God is not. While we are not protected from every difficulty, *God always holds us close.*

3. *Share the cellar.*

As our family rushed through the stormy night, our neighbors always held the big storm shelter door open for us. Descending the concrete stairs, we were greeted by the musty smells before we clumped together on benches in that dark, dank space. The storm roared overhead. What would our world look like when the sound stopped? God only knew. But sharing the experience with friends lessened the ferocity of the situation.

Trouble will come just like bad weather. The experience can grow our faith muscles, teach us life lessons, and deepen our character by the victorious grace of the Father.

— PRAYER —

God, be big in our lives. When storms dump on us, wreck our plans, and blot out the light, remind us that trouble always passes and faith-filled friends can lighten our load. And if we become afraid and don't know where to find shelter, carry us in Your loving arms. Amen.

THOUGHT FOR TODAY

God can pull us through the darkest hour.

Jane Jayroe is a former Miss America, television news anchor, and Oklahoma Cabinet Secretary of Tourism. She has co-authored an autobiography, More Grace than Glamour, *and* Oklahoma III.

Jane Jayroe

RELUCTANT CINDERELLA

But by the grace of God I am what I am, and His grace toward me was not in vain.

—1 Corinthians 15:10 NKJV

My inward life changed in one moment.

It was the moment I accepted that God created me to be someone beyond who I was on my own.

My outward life changed in one event.

I stood on a huge stage in Atlantic City, already stunned to have even reached the Miss America pageant, when suddenly, it was me who was being crowned, me smiling and walking the long runway. It should have been a dream come true, but it felt more like a nightmare come to life.

Have you ever faced a great opportunity and felt frozen in a sea of inadequacy? That was the feeling behind my smile. This winning moment felt more like a burden than a blessing.

The voices in my head screamed: you're not smart enough; you're not thin enough; you're not pretty enough; you're not good enough to be Miss America. You are just a kid from a little town in Oklahoma. What were the judges thinking? In 1966, the Miss America pageant was among the highest rated television shows on the air, and the title one of the most recognized in the world.

To say that I was unprepared for this moment was an understatement. I was nineteen years old, had never flown in an airplane, and had ridden to the competition with my schoolteacher parents. Even the Oklahoma pageant director hadn't come—although she had prepared me very well.

Nobody expected me to win—especially me. I was just thrilled to be there representing

Oklahoma and living my dream of walking the runway I had grown up watching on television.

While I struggled with fears of being left alone with these people in the foreign land of New Jersey, a miraculous grace note occurred.

From the moment I became Miss America, no phone call had been allowed into my hotel room. So, imagine my surprise on the day following the crowning, when the phone rang. I picked it up (another task against the rules) and a warm voice from my past reached out to deliver peace to my heart. It was Reverend Leonard Gillingham from Oklahoma—my family's favorite minister.

Leonard (as he insisted on being called) was such an effective servant of the Lord. He baptized my father and me together on a glorious Sunday evening in Sentinel, Oklahoma. He led us all into such a closer walk with God, and here he was again.

Whatever his words were in that moment, I couldn't recall, but what I experienced was grace. My internal trauma subsided because I knew when my parents left me in a few hours to go home, I would not be alone in New Jersey, New York, or any other place on earth.

Whether I was a success or failure for the next 365 days, I could be Miss America, because it wasn't up to me alone. *This wasn't about my ability to be perfect but my willingness to be faithful.* My dream had come true and by the grace of God, I was able to overcome my insecurities and accept it.

— PRAYER —

Forgive us when we doubt our dreams and deny our destiny. Remind us that You can transform any of us, if we're willing to step out of our comfortable spot. Call us beyond what we're capable of, Lord, and fill us with confidence in You. Amen.

THOUGHT FOR TODAY

Accept your dreams.

Coach Sherri Coale

THE RIPPLE

> *Cast your bread upon the waters, for after many days you will find it again.*
>
> —Ecclesiastes 11:1 NIV

When I was a little girl, I used to go pond fishing with my dad. He always fished with a plastic worm; I with a minnow and bobber. He would cast his line, effortlessly, way out into the middle of the pond, and I would splash mine, awkwardly, barely beyond the moss that glued the banks of red Oklahoma dirt to the muddy water that we worked diligently for fish. I would stand on the bank, my toes inches away from the water's edge, and watch the ripple race back to me only seconds following my chaotic cast. I would stand, likewise, waiting—and waiting and waiting—on the water's crawl following my dad's gentle toss. Funny thing was, no matter what, a ripple always came back.

I was mesmerized by that as a kid. I would watch the circle surrounding my dad's line expand and reach until it died into the earth under my toes. It happened every time. Every single time. How in the world could something so slight be so persistent? I used to marvel at it for hours, though I never really knew why. And then one day, long after I'd put that fishing pole away, I figured it out.

It was simple. Everything matters.

Every interaction that we have every single day makes an impact. It might be the way we answer the phone or the way we speak to the voice inside the box at the drive-through line at McDonald's. It might be the eye contact we make with the custodian at the office or the tone of our voice when we say, "Good morning," to our co-workers. What we do, what we say, how we say it—it all matters. We send out little waves that reach people and affect people in big and small ways. Constantly.

And the ripple always returns.

If we're really, really lucky, someone writes us a letter and tells us how we made a difference in their lives. But those are the bobber splashes, the big "you took me in when I had nowhere to go and, in so doing, changed my life" kind of ripples. Those happen more than we think, but they're not daily occurrences. More often the ripples come more subtly. They come in the form of a graduation announcement, or a Christmas card, or an invitation to a wedding. Just little ways in which people say, "You matter. You have impacted my life."

But mostly, the ripples happen slyly. They slip in and out of people's lives without the giver or the receiver really ever being aware of their significance. They arrive gently and sometimes only after a fair amount of time, like the slow, soft circles of the plastic worm. Those ripples might show up in the form of a job well done or word well kept. Or perhaps an individual simply walks a little taller or smiles a little broader because of how we made him feel. Sometimes people are just better versions of themselves because of something we did or said, and we, the world at large, are better for it.

— PRAYER —

Lord, thank You for the gift of making a difference in the lives of others. You call all of us to a life of meaning, to share what we've been given, and to encourage others. Remind us that You are the Source; we are Your hands that cast love into the lives of others. Amen.

THOUGHT FOR TODAY

Everything matters.

Sherri Coale is in her fourteenth season as head coach of the University of Oklahoma's women's basketball team. She is considered one of the top collegiate coaches in the nation. A native of Healdton, Oklahoma, Sherri spent her collegiate career playing for Oklahoma Christian University's basketball team where she was an Academic All-American.

First Lady Cathy Keating

FACING TRAGEDY

> *God is our refuge and strength, an ever-present help in trouble. Therefore we will not fear, though the earth give way and the mountains fall into the heart of the sea, though its waters roar and foam and the mountains quake of their surging.*
>
> —Psalm 46:1–3 NIV

April 19, 1995 is a day when the world stood still. The Alfred P. Murrah Federal Building in Oklahoma City was bombed, and it happened in our state's backyard. The act of terrorism brought our community, our state, and our nation to our knees. As a brand new First Lady, I wanted to help "right that wrong." I wanted to help our community heal.

But how? No playbook existed for a tragedy like this. I was new to public life and had no experience in such matters. For Oklahoma's sake, I could not fail. The answers I needed were obvious as I turned to my daily prayer since childhood—The Prayer of St. Francis of Assisi:

Lord, make me an instrument of your peace.
Where there is hatred, let me sow love;
where there is injury, pardon;
where there is doubt, faith;
where there is despair, hope;
where there is darkness, light;
and where there is sadness, joy.
O Divine Master, grant that I may not so
much seek to be consoled as to console;
to be understood as to understand;
to be loved as to love.
For it is in giving that we receive;
it is in pardoning that we are pardoned;
and it is in dying that we are born
to eternal life. Amen.

Now was the time to implement that prayer on a grand scale.

In a leap of faith, that April nineteenth night I began planning a prayer vigil with five friends, and "The Prayer Service" was born. Four days later our Oklahoma community came together while the world community joined in via television to begin our journey of healing through prayer. Just before the service, when the families of those injured or killed began to enter the Fairgrounds where the service was being held, my emotions overwhelmed me. I thought over and over that for them, *I cannot fail ... I must not fail.* However, I was experiencing much doubt.

At the service, Dr. Billy Graham inspired us to feel God's presence as He wrapped His arms around us in faith and lifted us from our knees to our feet. Dr. Graham stated, "Our knowledge is limited and there are some things we never understand this side of eternity. However, even though we do not understand, God does not change. He is still the God of love and mercy; and in the midst of our sorrow and pain, we can turn to Him in faith and trust." President Clinton assured us that America was strong and that the whole nation was standing with us in our grief. Frank, as Governor of Oklahoma, through his steady leadership, empathy, and compassion, conveyed that we would right this wrong and emphasized that we shared the heartache of all who had been affected.

That day, in our darkest hour, Oklahoma's journey of healing began in earnest and with an abundance of faith, hope, and love a community stood strong.

That leap of faith changed my life and I hope the lives of others.

— PRAYER —

God give us the strength, the courage, and the wisdom to do what is right. Amen.

THOUGHT FOR TODAY

A leap of faith can jump-start
a life-changing journey.

Cathy Keating is a former First Lady of Oklahoma and has a lifetime of community service. She has published three books: In Their Name, *a New York Times best seller;*

Our Governors' Mansions; *and* Ooh La La: Cuisine Presented in a Stately Manner. *Cathy is currently Chair of Philanthropy for Express Employment Professionals and serves on several national philanthropic boards.*

Justice Yvonne Kauger

ROLE MODEL

*Many daughters have done well, but you excel
them all.*

—Proverbs 31:29 NKJV

I first met my mother's oldest sister moments after
I was born. Lucille Margaret Bottom Simmons
was with my mother when, after a very difficult
labor, I was delivered with a breech presentation.
Mother wasn't doing so well, and they thought I
was dead. While the doctors tended to Mother,
Aunt Lucille turned her attention to me. She,
with her customary efficiency, exclaimed, "This
baby is alive!" That's the way I got my guardian
angel, surrogate mother, teacher, and role model.

We didn't have godmothers in our family, but she was mine.

She took me to the Methodist church where I discovered they had milk and cookies at Sunday School. I got to wear my bathrobe and be a shepherd in the Christmas play. This was particularly satisfying for me—no gender discrimination. Because I was a brunette, I had been rejected as an angel in the first grade. Angels could only be blonde; I had to be a star. (I now qualify as an angel insofar as the hair color is concerned.)

I was blessed with wonderful parents. My daddy always told me that I could do and be anything I wanted to, and my mother insisted that I do it right. Aunt Lucille exemplified their teaching. She was the first woman to be County Superintendent of Schools in Canadian County, and the first woman principal in Washita County. She could whip up an Easter suit overnight, make her own bread, weave baskets, and play basketball and piano. She made time for my sister and me to visit her in Stillwater in the summertime while she worked on her master's degree. (I got to shoot baskets in Gallagher Hall and meet

Uncle Henry's friend, the legendary coach, Mr. Iba.) After she graduated as valedictorian of her class at Lake Valley High School in 1920, she spent a summer at Southwestern State College. At seventeen, she rode her horse to teach at Star, a little one-room school. After a lifetime of teaching in Oklahoma's public schools, she retired. But she wasn't finished; she had just started. She learned to ride a bicycle and speak Swahili at age sixty-five. She served two terms in the Peace Corps in Kenya and Tanzania. Africa was the highlight of her career.

She came back to Weatherford and cared for my grandmother until she could not lift her anymore. She nursed Uncle Henry until he died, and she continued to teach people to read, this time immigrants—Chinese and Hispanic. Her pupils opened restaurants in town, and she was greeted with glee and profuse appreciation when she frequented them. She still played piano. From the time she was an octogenarian, she went to the nursing home to play for the "old people."

She continued to bake bread every week with loaves for sharing, too. Then she met the former dean of men at Southwestern Oklahoma State

University, cookie-baking, golf-playing George, the love of her life. They got married in El Reno when she was eighty-five. Mr. and Mrs. George Ryden shook hands when they were pronounced husband and wife, and they lived happily-ever-after for ten years, the best time of her life. So maybe there is hope for me. Thank God for Aunt Lucille. She did it right!

— PRAYER —

Almighty and ever living God, source of all wisdom and understanding, be present with us. Guide us to perceive what is right, and grant us both the courage to pursue it and the grace to accomplish it. Amen.

THOUGHT FOR TODAY

Try to do it right.

Yvonne Kauger is a former cotton-picking-cotton chopper, hay hauler, part-time secretary, medical technologist, and graduate of the Oklahoma City University night law school. She was chosen by Justice Ralph Hodges as the first woman staff lawyer for the Oklahoma Supreme Court and was the second woman appointed to the Oklahoma Supreme Court and the only woman to have served as Vice Chief Justice and Chief Justice of that Court. (Her parents, John and Alice Kauger, and her Aunt Lucille were present when Justice Hodges administered her oath of office on March 22, 1984.)

Jane Jayroe

GRACE LESSONS

Let us then approach the throne of grace with confidence, so that we may receive mercy and find grace to help us in our time of need.
—Hebrews 4:16 NIV

In the first grade, I broke a rule. Students were instructed not to wade in mud puddles. Wandering around outside in my brand new coat, I was drawn to a small pool of brown water. Splashing was fun until my boot hit a rock, and I fell face first into the leftover rain runoff. Covered head to toe with mud, there was no hiding what I had done.

I stood in that dirty coat with my head held low, facing my teacher, Miss Thomas. My punishment was to stay in from recess for two weeks. Worse than anything was the feeling I had disappointed my loving and kind teacher.

After a few days of sitting at my desk while other kids were outside playing, Miss Thomas asked me to help her with a project. I loved working close to her, and the sun began to shine again as I felt her affirmation in spite of my mistake.

It felt bad to have broken the rule, and I missed going outside with my friends; but it was comforting to know that I was loved in spite of doing the wrong thing and to think that after paying the price I could start over with a clean slate. It was a welcome lesson. Mother called it "grace."

Since those early years, I have fallen into much deeper murky water. But always I've found grace. A loving God has forgiven my wrong choices and found a way to use my bad decisions for good lessons.

— PRAYER —

Lord, all of us mess up but only You can cover the mistakes with mercy and grace. Help us to make good choices and lead righteous lives. But when we stumble, remind us to approach Your throne of grace with confidence. Amen.

THOUGHT FOR TODAY

Messy mistakes can be made clean.

LEARNING STEWARDSHIP OF GIFTS

The Spirit has given each of us a special way of serving others.

—1 Corinthians 12: 7 CEV

Like most students in high school, I loved to hang out with my friends or watch television, but in our household, we went to choir practice at the church every Wednesday night.

"But Mother," I wailed, "none of my friends have to do something so stupid."

"You're going," she said with that warm smile that made it hard to be mad at her.

I stomped out to the car and slammed the car door. "You can make me go," I pouted, "but you can't make me *want* to go."

Mother put our blue Buick in gear, and off we went down Main Street in the cold night. Passing the high school on the right, the football field on the left, we saw the only stoplight in town ahead, blinking red.

We pulled into the church parking lot next to a few others.

I gave it one more try. "Everybody here is old. Why do I have to be the only kid who comes?"

Mother switched the car off and turned to me. "Janie, you know that argument doesn't mean a thing to me. You have received a gift, and it's up to you to develop it and use it in service to others. You sing so well, there's nobody I would rather hear than you and your sister." Lucky for my dear sibling, she had fled the coop to college.

I heard my mom's message, but I didn't like it, except that part about being a good singer.

Inside the sanctuary, my resentment faded. The church felt warm in ways not just physical; the other folks were so kind. And singing, after all, was my joy. Even with that woman on the organ who played the keyboard with one hand

and directed us with the other, singing praises to God felt somehow right.

In my family, it didn't matter that you made the top grades, won the highest award, or were the star athlete; being a good steward of what you'd been given was the goal. It wasn't a question of being responsible *for* our gifts, rather that we were responsible *to* Someone for what we'd been given. We were response-able because of God.

Those lessons learned growing up in little Laverne, Oklahoma, have served me well. Whatever success has come my way has been the result of God-given abilities plus hard work. We don't need to judge our gifts … just develop them and let them be an offering.

— PRAYER —

Thank You, Lord, for the many gifts You have provided. Forgive us for wanting to trade some in for others or just being ungrateful or forgetful of what has been given. You are the potter; we are the clay. Mold us to Your glory and purpose. Amen.

THOUGHT FOR TODAY

God has gifted each of us.

LaDonna Meinders

THE HUMILITY OF SIDEWALK SWEEPING

For everyone who exalts himself will be humbled, and he who humbles himself will be exalted.
—Luke 14:11 NIV

After twenty-three years of marriage, I found myself facing a divorce. I had been a stay-at-home mom, which I came to recognize as a genuine luxury. Other than teaching piano, I had never had a job, and now, at just over forty, I faced the terrifying prospect of job-hunting.

I applied at the local newspaper and was delighted to get a job proofreading and selling ads.

It was not easy. Proofreading was more demanding than casual reading, as I learned the hard way when the editor called me in and showed me some glaring mistakes in a front-page headline. And selling ads to the local businesspeople in our small town, most of whom I had known for years in social situations, took courage. It was hard not to feel personally rejected if a friend didn't take out a big ad! Then there was the matter of working with, and for, people who were much younger than I. But the most difficult thing for me, and probably the thing that taught me the most valuable lesson, was when it came my turn to sweep the sidewalk in front of the newspaper office.

Each of us has a certain image of ourselves, and sometimes it's not very accurate. Mine was shaped by many things: I had been Miss Oklahoma; I had a college degree; my husband had been in politics; and we had socialized with governors and senators. Not only that, but I think our family had an exaggerated idea of our importance in our small town. My face burned with humiliation as I took the broom and headed out the front door of the newspaper office. I did the job as quickly as I could, hoping none of my friends would see me. I felt the same when it was my turn to fill the newspaper dispenser at the supermarket, where the entire town seemed to be going in and out.

I survived the job and the divorce, and I learned a lot. As I gradually overcame my sensitivity, I began to see things in perspective. I learned that being older doesn't necessarily mean being smarter. I learned that punching a time clock was okay, and that it felt good to pick up my check and pay bills. I developed a sense of humor and was able to laugh at myself.

As I moved on to better-paying jobs, I realized that they had more prestige, but my actual work was no more honorable than when I had been asked to sweep the sidewalk. Every job is important! When we are too full of ourselves, it's hard to think of ourselves as team players.

I think I am wiser and more compassionate because of these important experiences. I will always be grateful to the newspaper publisher who hired me, green as grass, for that first job.

God has a plan for your life and mine, and we can fulfill that plan if we don't let pride hold us back. But don't pray for humility unless you are ready to use that broom and do whatever task He has in mind for you.

— PRAYER —

Lord, I confess my pride. Perhaps it's because I feel inadequate or afraid that I tend to act important. Help me to walk in humility even as Christ was humble and made Himself a servant to others. In His name I pray. Amen.

THOUGHT FOR TODAY

Practice humility today for a gracious tomorrow.

LaDonna Meinders is a church and civic leader. She is an accomplished musician and author of Leaves in the Wind, Angel Hugs, _and_ Angel Hugs for Cancer Patients. _LaDonna and her husband, Herman, are philanthropists and supporters of many worthy causes._

Jane Thompson

COURAGE THROUGH DIFFICULT TIMES

God did not give us a spirit of timidity, but a spirit of power, of love and of self-discipline.
—II Timothy 1:7 NIV

There I was, sitting in the doctor's office waiting for his opinion on a recently detected lump on my mandible (jawbone). As a fifteen-year survivor of head and neck cancer this was not my first time with a potential problem. I had experienced this moment on three previous occasions. What made this time different, however, was that I was pregnant with our third child. I realized my life might never be the same.

To my surprise, my husband arrived in the office. He had been summoned by the doctor. We listened to the description of the recommended course of action: abort the child, remove the tumor and half of my mandible, remove most of my tongue, and live with major facial disfigurement for the rest of my life. The doctor stated the outcome might not be desired, but it was a matter of life and death. He continued by reminding us that after all, we had the perfect family—a girl and a boy. His bedside manners were atrocious. While picking up the phone to schedule the abortion, he explained that the tumor was a fast growing cancer and must be removed immediately.

I had never considered myself to be a weak person; however, it was not my nature to question the professional advice of a physician. With tears streaming down my face, I went inside my heart where I surrendered my decision to my Lord and Savior. After a long pause, I felt an answer to my prayer. With more peace than I could have imagined, I simply stated: "I will not abort this child. I will get a second, third, and fourth opinion if necessary to determine the right course of action that will enable this child to live." My loving husband agreed, and we walked out of the room knowing our resolve was spiritually inspired and the Lord would not place a burden on either of us we couldn't handle.

Not knowing where our journey would take us, we had confidence that the final outcome would be God's will. We consulted with three doctors, each with differing opinions, and I selected the course of treatment that would be most favorable to the birth of a healthy baby.

That was twenty-three years ago, and today we have a most beautiful daughter whom we love very much. I personally have been in remission for eighteen years and lead a very active life.

There is not a day in my life that I don't reflect on the scripture II Timothy 1:7. Through our faith, He gives us strength, confidence, a deep appreciation for love and self-discipline.

Respect professional caregivers, but trust God to guide you to the right decision.

— PRAYER —

Dear Lord, thank You for Your loving grace, guidance, and healing. Thank You for being the solid rock for us to hold onto in difficult times. We praise You for giving us strength, power, love, and self-discipline. Amen.

THOUGHT FOR TODAY

Ask God for courage to overcome difficulties.

Jane Thompson is a prominent community leader and volunteer. She is married to the newspaper publisher of The Oklahoman, *David Thompson. Together they enjoy their two daughters, son, and grandchildren. Jane has inspired many with her willingness to live in a courageous way.*

Linda Cavanaugh

FOR THE LOVE
OF LAUGHTER

A cheerful heart is good medicine.
—Proverbs 17:22 NIV

What I remember most about the arena was its size. It was much larger than I expected—a fitting stage for an event that had drawn people from hundreds of miles away for this traditional Indian powwow. Little did I know that what was about to unfold in the next ten minutes would teach me one of life's lessons not easily forgotten.

I was there on that hot, summer evening to produce a series of television reports on

Oklahoma's Native American culture. I had been forewarned that if an elder asked me to dance, that it would be considered bad form to decline.

That made me nervous.

The fact is that I can't dance. Never could. I'm a woman who apparently lacks the gene that allows one's body to move in a beautifully rhythmic way to music. I'd long ago given up trying.

That's when I felt a gentle tap on my shoulder. I turned around to face one of the tribe's elders. He gently motioned me to the head of the line forming for the dance. I tried to explain as we walked to the center of the arena that I was grateful for his invitation, but feared he had made a bad choice for a partner.

"It's very easy," he said. "Simply do what she does." He pointed to the Indian princess standing in front of me.

As the sound of the drums began to vibrate throughout the building, I watched, as she seemed to dip with each beat.

She'd take a step with her right foot, and then dip on her left. Step, dip. Step dip.

I followed her example. She'd step. I'd step. She'd dip. I'd dip.

Perfect.

I felt an unusual sense of accomplishment as the dancers made their way around the arena. *I'm actually dancing*, I thought with pride.

By the time the traditional song had ended and the last echo of the drum had faded, I was thrilled.

I shook hands with my partner and with the lady whose example I'd been following. Then, she turned and walked away—with a noticeable limp.

She had a broken leg.

Her cast had been covered by a full-length buckskin dress and traditional leggings. I had been limping around the arena just as she did.

— PRAYER —

Heavenly Father, never let me lose the ability to laugh at myself. When I'm tempted to take myself too seriously, help me recall those moments when I was foolish. And let me smile. Amen.

THOUGHT FOR TODAY

Bless me with laughter this day.

Linda Cavanaugh is an award winning broadcast journalist, having been honored with fifteen Emmys. Linda has been a television news anchor for thirty-two years and has led the field in telling important stories. Linda is also an author and speaker.

Jane Jayroe

THE ART
OF GRATEFULNESS

> *Do not be anxious about anything, but in every-thing, by prayer and petition, with thanksgiving, present your requests to God.*
> —Philippians 4:6 NIV

My stomach was churning as I drove round and round in the big concrete lot in the Oklahoma State Capitol complex looking for a place to park my car. This was my first day on the job for the State Department of Education, and it was a day of conflicting emotions for me. On one hand, I was grateful to have a job because I was desperate for a salary and benefits. On the other, I was embarrassed that after being the queen of the hop as Miss America ten years earlier, a divorce had brought me to a really low spot on the road. Surely people had expected me to be a movie star or something highly successful after such a stunning start at nineteen, but here I was, broke and divorced with a new baby and a job that my dad had helped me get.

As I walked up the steps into this cold government building, I was thinking of the emotional and spiritual work that had brought me to this point and out of the hole of depression. It had not been easy. I had spent months being angry, full of self-pity, and shaking my fist at God for the unfairness of my situation. But at last, I had a job to pay the rent. Being desperate and alone with a new baby was humbling.

On this bright Oklahoma morning, with an apprehensive feeling in my gut, I *decided* to be grateful for what was rather than what could have been. Having a daily routine, a small but reliable salary, and a pleasant work environment was a gift of grace.

Before long, I saw that choosing an attitude of gratitude helped create positive work relationships and eventually led to a career opportunity that was to be my destiny—television news.

Being thankful draws good things to us and is a remarkable anti-depressant. Attempting to be appreciative in all things is not about being a Pollyanna with our head in the sand; it's about trusting that beneath the surface of circumstances is a good God. With a grace-filled vision every day, we can recognize His hand. Maybe it's a caring nurse, a beautiful day, a telephone call from a friend, a tasty bit of food, a well-written book, a lick from a loving dog—every twenty-four hours can prompt some thankfulness.

In prayer and in journaling, I ask myself, how can I reframe my vision in order to develop a grateful heart? Recognizing those doses of goodness softens the hard lines of life and lifts the spirit.

— PRAYER —

God of abundance, thank You for the blessings of this day. For our country, our community, our friends, and Your love—we give thanks. Let our hearts learn gratitude as we receive gifts and acknowledge You as the Giver. Amen.

THOUGHT FOR TODAY

Gratitude nurtures an awareness of God.

GIVEN ENOUGH

David took off the [King Saul's] armor and picked up his shepherd's stick.

—1 Samuel 17:39–40 CEV

When I received the opportunity to co-anchor the prime time news in Dallas/Ft. Worth, Texas, I was ecstatic…and nervous. Immediately, I began plotting how I could change myself to insure success in a top-ten television market. I must become hard-hitting, aggressive, and confident. My appearance should smack not of a glamorous girl but a serious journalist.

I made an appointment with my pastor, Dr. Norman Neaves, to discuss this life change. As I began sharing with him my vision of who I should become, he looked at me with intensity. "You have everything you need to be successful," he said. "But it's important to be authentic to who you are."

Norman's words were ringing true to my history.

"You are smart enough to study the way other people act and mimic them," he said, "but you will always feel afraid of being found out. Your strength comes from who God made you to be."

I wasn't so sure. After accepting this career challenge, I moved to Texas. My early performance on television reflected my desire to be taken seriously. I wore dark suits, cut my hair short, and minimized my makeup.

After a few months, my news director called me in. He said their research on me was positive except for one thing. "You are too serious," he said. "Just be yourself and relax."

I did. Success followed, and the joy of doing my job increased tremendously. Like David of the Old Testament, I wasn't going to be my best wearing someone else's armor. When David prepared to face the giant, Goliath, Saul dressed the young boy in the King's finest gear. But

David refused it. Instead, he chose two reliable weapons: trust in God and his shepherd's sling.

In my life's professional calling, God had blessed me with an intense interest in a variety of subjects, a love of storytelling, calm nerves under pressure, and an ease with reading on a teleprompter.

Like David, I, too, had been given everything I needed to achieve my career goals. I didn't have to be totally confident in myself, just confident in the One who made me.

— PRAYER —

Lord, thank You for making me just as I am. Forgive me when I question Your creation and make a career of finding fault with it. Help me trust You in all things. Amen.

THOUGHT FOR TODAY

God has provided everything we need.

Bobbie Roe

SOFTLY AND TENDERLY, JESUS IS CALLING

Jesus said to her, "Woman, why are you weeping? Whom are you looking for?"

—John 20:15 NRSV

In summer 1993, my mother suddenly died of an aneurysm shortly after the death of my stepfather. For weeks afterwards, I wept and grieved inconsolably. Guilt shrouded my heart, as I remembered all the times that I hadn't visited or even called to say, "I love you," because I was just too busy. Unable to breathe within the confines of my house, I began to spend long days in the yard, digging small gardens out of hard clay and withered grass. Then, one fall day, my neighbor Olivia saw me laboring in the dirt. For seventeen years, we had only occasionally waved to each other, but that day she came across the street and asked, "Bobbie, would you like to walk with me?"

In the following weeks, we walked many miles together. During our journeys, we talked about the deserts, as well as the gardens, of our lives. But even in the deserts of her life, Olivia knew that Jesus had always been near; He had restored those dry, lifeless places with His redeeming grace and love. As I listened to her faith story, something in her soft, tender words began to touch the hard and withered places within me.

Near Easter, as I tended the glorious flowers that had risen out of grief's labors, a joyous refrain suddenly rose from my soul: "Christ is in my heart, and I joy to toil in the garden of the Lord!" As the words sang forth again and again, I began to feel what Mary Magdalene must have felt when she realized that the One whom she had mistaken for an ordinary gardener was really Jesus, her living God. Like Mary Magdalene,

I had been so blinded by grief that I could not see my risen Lord right beside me. But in the midst of loss and suffering, Jesus had always been nearby, softly and tenderly calling, "Bobbie! Why are you weeping? Whom are you looking for? Would you like to walk with me?"

— PRAYER —

Loving God, thank You for calling us out of darkness to walk in faith with You. Amen.

THOUGHT FOR TODAY

Into whose life is Christ calling you today?

Bobbie Roe, Ph.D., is a retreat leader and spiritual director. She is a member of Church of the Servant in Oklahoma City. In 2001, Bobbie and her husband, Tom, cofounded Broken Bread retreat ministry. They have two adult sons, Tyler and Todd.

Charlotte Lankard

THANKSLIVING

In everything give thanks: for this is the will of God in Christ Jesus concerning you.
—1 Thessalonians 5:18 KJV

"Count your blessings, name them one by one, and it will surprise you what the Lord has done."

These are words to a hymn that I heard on a regular basis growing up as a preacher's kid. Gratitude was a daily part of the home in which I was raised and was always present, even in the midst of difficulties.

The word gratitude was made bigger for me many years ago by my friend, entertainer, and theologian Grady Nutt, who was killed in a plane crash in 1982.

Grady left a legacy of stories that continue to enrich my life. One is titled *Thanksliving*.

Thanksliving was prompted by an encounter with Wesley Alexander, who was seated next to Grady on an airplane. Wesley was a high school senior on spring vacation who wanted to be a psychiatrist to "help people's minds."

During their conversation, Grady asked, "You have any hobbies?"

"Just doin' it," was the answer. When Grady asked what he meant, he said, "You know ... just bein'."

Grady said he hadn't had such a sneaky blessing in a long time, a blessing that spoke to him of a special attitude.

"Just being ... his hobby!" *Just bein'!* Thus *Thanksliving* was born into a book titled *Agaperos* by Grady Nutt.

Thanksliving was defined for us as an *attitude that finds treasure in the plowed field of routine ... that sees daily bread as a provision of the Bread of life ... that holds a cup to the water of life and drinks the mystery of being with zest.*

Thanksliving. An eye for perspective, for color, harmony and balance ... that sees how "all things work together for good to them who love God"... who find in life that God loves them.

Thanksliving. An ear for the cry of pain, the laugh of joy, the dirge of woe, and the lyric of delight... the hollow echo of lonely, the vibes of together, the whisper of help, and the shout of love.

Thanksliving. A touch for appropriate, for right, for compassion, for care, for simpatico, for grief, for anger, for all meaningful deep feeling.

Thanksgiving. Seeing, hearing, feeling the "God-with-us" in simple truth, in complexity: an umbrella in rain/a convertible in sun... wool for a sheep in winter and shears in spring... salt on meat and sugar in tea... coping and hoping.

Thanksliving. Seeing that the beauty of life is in its pace, direction, movement, ebb, and now... falling in line with its current... conquering in adversity... rejoicing in joyful splendor.

Thanksliving. To live and give, to "do it..." to make a "hobby of being."

— PRAYER —

As we live our lives—"*just bein'*"—offering what we have that is useful, celebrating the good and moving through the challenging times of adversity—may we be *Thanksliving* women, counting our blessings each day, regardless of circumstances. Amen.

THOUGHT FOR TODAY

Help me be thankful today.

Charlotte Lankard is a weekly columnist for The Oklahoman, *the state's largest newspaper. She is a licensed marriage and family therapist; founder of Calm Waters, support groups for grieving children; and former director of the James Hall Jr. Center for Mind, Body, and Spirit at Integris Health. She is author of* It's Called Life, *and a noted speaker.*

Barbara Green

LISTENING
FOR GOD'S VOICE

...And His sheep follow Him because they know His voice.

—John 10:4 NIV

David and I married at an early age—he was nineteen; I was seventeen. We had grown up in a small town set in the middle of cotton fields and cattle ranches. From the beginning, we felt the Lord in our relationship.

When David was a junior in high school, he fell in love with retail business. As a young bride, I accepted his dream to be a shared calling. For several years my husband worked for a five-and-dime chain of stores called TG&Y. During that time our family grew to include three children.

In 1970, we stepped out in faith. With a 600 dollar loan from the bank, we started a picture framing business. David kept his day job while we all worked at our kitchen table to make miniature picture frames. It was a family effort—we paid the little guys seven cents a frame.

Thus Hobby Lobby was born. Today there are 434 stores in thirty-five states.

Whenever we have faced decisions, David and I have listened for God's voice. Our choices have not always been easy. In 1986, our company was in serious trouble. We called our family together and prayed for God's guidance. Our oldest son, Mart, told his dad, "It's okay. Our faith is not in you—it's in God. If we lose the businesses, we'll still be okay."

We were reminded once again of our priorities—God first, family second, and work third.

Another challenge faced our family in 1998, when we struggled with being open for business on Sunday. At this time, we had stores in eight states. Our sales-per-hour were highest on

Sunday—one hundred million dollars a year. After much prayer and reflection, we felt the Lord speaking to us about the sanctity of church and setting aside a day of rest for our families.

We began that change with three stores in Nebraska. Sales numbers immediately took a dip. The closures brought a lot of attention from the press; we were going against retail trends.

As we read reports in the newspapers of our actions, we were shaken. It sounded like we were determined to close on Sunday in order to be obedient to our principles *only* if it worked out financially in Nebraska.

It was as if God was saying directly to us: "Oh, so if you're blessed, you're going to be obedient? But if the numbers don't work out for you, then maybe not?"

We made the decision to close *all* our stores on Sunday. It took some time but by the year 2000, Hobby Lobby had ceased to be open for business that one day in Nebraska, Oklahoma, Alabama, Kansas, Arkansas, Missouri, Colorado, and Texas.

A curious thing happened after that drop in business in Nebraska. The sales volumes began rebounding to their previous levels, and kept climbing.

In all situations, we believe in seeking God's voice. Responding in obedience is our goal. The measure of our lives is not how much we accumulate, but rather the way in which we align ourselves with God's purposes.

— PRAYER —

Lord, thank You for grounding our lives in scripture, prayer, and church. You are our Shepherd speaking to us in love and offering direction. Amen.

THOUGHT FOR TODAY

Seek God in everything.

Barbara and David Green founded Hobby Lobby. The story is told in David's book, More Than a Hobby. *They have three children, ten grandchildren, and one great grandchild. The Green family supports many Christian charities. Among their favorites is City Rescue Mission in Oklahoma City. Barbara chaired the campaign that built a new facility for the homeless. She remains active on their board today.*

Jane Jayroe

EDITH'S STORY

She did what she could.

—Mark 14:8 NIV

Edith taught me a lot about joy generated from an attitude of service.

I met her on a sparkling spring day. My photographer and I dragged our television equipment toward her house that was almost hidden behind other homes. We had come to this inner city neighborhood to shoot a story for our series on volunteers. Our destination home was set back from the street and looked as though it had grown out of a garage. The structure was so small that I worried that our equipment wouldn't fit within the walls.

The porch was sitting on the front of the house like a swollen lower lip and was decorated with wind chimes and saucers filled with cat food. Pots of flowers were scattered about. For a minute, this felt like a fairy tale. Who was this woman we were meeting?

The door opened and my eyes dropped to meet Edith. She only came to my waist even though we were of similar height. Edith suffered from arthritis and was so debilitated by it that she couldn't stand. Her home was too small for a wheelchair so she had designed her own transportation: a piece of plywood on wheels with a pillow strapped on top. She had folded herself on the self-designed scooter. Now she zipped around propelled by strong arms and hands.

This was no ordinary woman. Her warm smile wrapped us in a spirit that touched my core and changed my perspective. Edith was a dynamo of service to nonprofit organizations in our community. Before retirement, she had been a secretary. Now she offered her skills of sorting, stuffing, and mailing to several groups. She explained how she worked.

"This is where I lay the stacks out and put them together," she said proudly, pointing to a sofa that also served as her bed. "I love it when Debbie (the volunteer coordinator) comes to pick them up when I'm finished."

"My daughter wants me to move to California to be near her," she said, "but I told her that this is my spot."

We left Edith's house with a memorable story under our belts. "My spot," she had said. *This community is my spot, too,* I thought. It has so many needs but is blessed with so many positive people like Edith.

I wrote and delivered many stories during my seventeen-year career in television news, but this one stays within my heart, especially on days when I'm tempted to whine about my life.

"There's always a need to fill and someone to help," I can hear Edith saying. She taught many of us that joy is a byproduct of purpose and service to others.

— PRAYER —

Thank You for Edith, Lord, and all those who remind us how we can serve one another. Bless her simple spirit, courage, and generosity. Help me be more like her today. Amen.

THOUGHT FOR TODAY

Joy comes in giving.

THE BEAUTY
OF GRACE

And let the beauty of the Lord our God be upon us, and establish the work of our hands for us.
—Psalm 90:17 NKJV

One morning I woke up with a stranger's arm on my pillow. It couldn't belong to me. The skin was crepey, and the veins showed through the loose skin. The appendage was attached to my shoulder even though it had mysteriously changed to look like my mother's.

Beginning at the age of forty, most of us watch, with amazement, if not horror, the aging process that alters our attractiveness. Everything seems to change—and not gracefully: sight dims, hearing fails, wrinkles multiply, medical concerns heighten, and most body parts fall. It's not a pretty picture.

When five thousand women were asked about their own beauty, over 54 percent of them said they were unhappy with their ankles. Responses went downhill from there.

While most of us are never satisfied with our measure of prettiness compared to our culture's standards, some of us learn to dig deeper for a definition of lasting beauty.

When I asked a class of three hundred women to write down whom they considered beautiful in their lives—all lifted up women who were loving, like a mother or grandmother. Their appearances were hardly considered. It confirmed the fact that unforgettable beauty is a face that looks at yours with unconditional love. It's a hand that serves, a mind that is wise, a nature that shares joy and laughter, and a heart that is full.

We are so much more than what looks back from the mirror. Each day challenges us to be grateful for that image and what it represents—

our history, our health, and our individual gifts. We strive to be good stewards of our appearance, but the beauty that speaks grace to others is not just external—it's deep down good.

— PRAYER —

Lord, because of Your grace, we know that it matters more how we live than how we look. Whom we love more than whom we know. And what we offer more than what we own. Amen.

THOUGHT FOR TODAY

Thank God for our true beauty.

Robin Marsh

THE 'F' WORD: FORGIVENESS

> ... *that no root of bitterness springing up causes trouble, and by it many be defiled* ...
> —Hebrews 12:15 NASB

It offended me like a four-letter word. My heart pounded and my head started spinning trying to comprehend what I was hearing. What foreign language was she speaking? Healing my broken heart meant forgiving? This was the last thing I wanted to hear! "Don't you know that I'm in the depths of despair?" At this point for me, healing had the face of revenge!

In the blink of an eye, my marriage was over! If divorce had never been an option in my life, how did I find myself losing what meant the most to me? My husband, my family, and our marriage ministry were destroyed. Fear fought to rule my life! I pleaded, "Father, help me survive! Help me breathe! Help me live!" I found out fast God's Word was my lifeline.

What about that "F" word? Forgiveness. Did it have to be complete?

Yes, God showed me. I could forgive my ex-husband, but that other person? My wise friend encouraged me to buy her a gift. So I prayed, "Lord, show me how to forgive those I don't love."

This gift was on my mind for several months. Out shopping one day I found a beautiful turquoise necklace, and I bought it for myself. But something miraculous happened when I went to place it around my neck. *This is the gift,* I heard. It sounded like a secret being whispered in my ear. Then I heard it again, *This is the gift,* but this time with more clarity.

God was leading me down the path of forgiveness and it was my turn to walk in obedience.

Face to face with the person I never wanted to forgive, the Lord let me see her in a new light. Gently, I placed the turquoise necklace in her hands and said, "You do a lot for my son when I cannot be there. I am grateful. I hope you receive this gift in the spirit it is given."

God is so good. He gave us the greatest gift of forgiveness. His Son Jesus died on the cross so that we could be forgiven and have eternal life. His Word tells us over and over again to forgive so our bitterness will not defile those we love. In Matthew, chapter 18 when Peter the disciple asked, "How many times do I forgive my brother?" Jesus answered in verse 22, "I do not say to you up to seven times, but up to seventy times seven." That comes out to 490. God showed me that meant to forgive daily even for the remembrance of the offense.

Forgiveness changed my life. I wish I had done it sooner. It allowed me to take the rope off my own neck and breathe in the abundant life God's Word shows us we can have.

The "F" word—forgiveness. Now I know it does mean a four-letter word—*free*. God's freedom giving us the power to do what is right instead of what we want.

— PRAYER —

Lord, give me the grace to forgive as I have been forgiven. Take the bitterness in my heart and give me peace. Remind me that when I don't forgive, I hurt myself more than any other. Amen.

THOUGHT FOR TODAY

Forgive someone today.

Robin Marsh is a national award winning television journalist, motivational speaker, and happily married mom.

Dr. Susan Chambers

NEIGHBORLY LOVE

You shall love your neighbor as yourself.
—Matthew 22:39 NKJV

I am a have: *h-a-v-e*. I like being a *have*. I'm grateful for being a *have*.

I *have* a wonderful family starting with wonderful parents, grandparents, and a brother. I have lots of childhood memories.

I *have* a wonderful husband who puts up with me, and three children who claim to still love me.

I *have* benefited from an education that has challenged me and encouraged me to be more than I ever thought I could be.

I *have* a job I love (except at two in the morning) and professional partners who truly care about the health of women.

I *have* a church that I can freely attend that helps me grow on my faith journey.

I *have* friends who are fun. Loyal. Best buds.

I *have* books to read, movies to watch, season tickets to sporting events, more Halloween decorations than most people can imagine, and a step counter I wear so I dutifully take at least ten thousand steps a day. I *have* a pantry and a fridge full of food, a babysitter who has helped me care for my kids for twenty years, a big front porch from which to watch spring storms, and a car with a full tank of gas—I am embarrassingly and gratefully a *have*.

But until I became involved with World Neighbors and they opened my eyes to the world, I was not *really* a *have* ... now I am.

World Neighbors works around the globe to eradicate hunger, poverty, and disease. On my visits to their communities I met women who truly live at the end of the road. They are desperately poor and living on less than a dollar a day. These women were grateful we were there to care about them, treat them with dignity, and promise our support so that they can continue to improve their lives and have hope for their children's future.

These women seemed to be light-years away from us, yet we have so much in common. I'm reminded of a trip to Mali. I left my patients and my family for three and a half weeks. I was not worried about my patients because amazing partners and nurses cared for them. However, my family was something else.

In one Mali village, we became well acquainted with the women. There were twelve American women in our group. We had our closing session sitting under a huge baobab tree. It always took awhile to converse, as it had to go from English to French to the local dialect and back again. One of the African women asked us if we had families.

"Yes," we answered.

"So, who is taking care of them while you are here on the other side of the world?" she asked.

"Our husbands," we responded.

They *gasped!*

Although it was very funny, I said to myself, "Oh yeah, we women are *all* on the same page—

always the caregivers, the organizers, the glue that holds it all together. We are the core of the family; the worriers for the family." I was certain at that moment my kids probably had not brushed their teeth in two weeks. I think the African women wondered if our families were still in one piece.

I have and cherish a million life-changing stories from World Neighbors. I have gained so much by sharing my life with people all over the world. Now I know what it means to *have* neighbors.

The founder of World Neighbors, John Peters, issued this challenge to all of us as he stood before the congregation of St. Luke's Methodist Church in 1951: "Let no man say, why don't they do something? There is no *they;* there is just us, you and me—free men and women, responsible individuals."

— PRAYER —

Lord, let us never forget others. Let us never be so comfortable that we fail to share. Give us the privilege of being our brother and our sister's keeper. Amen.

THOUGHT FOR TODAY

Help me love my neighbor, near and far.

Susan Chambers, a practicing obstetrician/ gynecologist in Oklahoma City, is a dedicated World Neighbors volunteer, former board member, and board chairperson. World Neighbors is an international development organization working to eradicate hunger, poverty, and disease in Asia, Africa, and Latin America.

Kay Murcer

BLUEPRINTS FOR OUR SEASONS OF CHANGE

There is a time for everything, and a season for every activity under heaven ... a time to tear down and a time to build.

—Ecclesiastes 3:1–3 NIV

I have boulders on my shoulders where my bra straps ought to be.

Who'd have thought I'd have to carry so much scary "death debris"?

I never guessed the very best of who I was would disappear.

I miss the me I used to be, but she's been gone now for a year.

A year after my husband, Bobby, died, I cried and mourned the loss of who I'd never be again—the *me* that had only been possible because *we* were together, high school sweethearts married for forty-two years. It had taken a full year without him for me to fully understand the enormity of this hole left behind once "my giant oak" had fallen, uprooting the life we had shared. That cavernous void was calling me to instantly take on a role I was comfortable only co-starring in. I did not want to be solely responsible for every financial, legal, and medical decision made for our household—my household. It was overwhelming.

I'd reached my sixtieth birthday just before Bobby's death, and fully knew how blessed my life had always been. In fact, through the bleakest days following his diagnosis, little miracles arrived in abundance, providing a peace that calmed all our fears. Now I needed to look to God's Word, our atlas of faith that had maneuvered us over cancer's bumpy road for two years. Disney World may provide incredible maps to help guests find their way to the Magic Kingdom, but they can't compare to God's map. It led us on a journey of peace toward His kingdom, and I now knew He would plot my course and help me build the bridge necessary to move forward. God's message let me look at that dark place and see His light on the other side.

I'm now in a rebuilding process; a period of adjustment I imagine will take years to fully blossom. Family and friends keep me in their prayers. They give an inexhaustible amount of support and love I feed from. I realize how blessed I am and I recognize the deep spiritual growth Bobby and I experienced as a result of life's cycles. The barriers we encountered were opportunities for God's light to shine through if we let it. I'm still praying daily for God's glow to emanate from my heart—it's my beacon of faith, my prism of God's love.

— PRAYER —

Continue to use us, dear Lord, as lamps of Your light to the world. Guide us through all the obstacles of life, presenting us with solutions to build new paths toward Your heavenly home … reuniting us with loved ones now in Your care. Amen.

THOUGHT FOR TODAY

A daily dose of God's word can recharge your batteries for life.

Kay Murcer is a courageous supporter of cancer charities. She was married to New York Yankee baseball great and announcer, Bobby Murcer. She worked with Bobby on his book, Yankee For Life. *She has two children and five grandchildren.*

Jane Jayroe

REWARDING RISKS

He guarded him ... like an eagle that stirs up its nest and hovers over its young, that spreads its wings to catch them and carries them on its pinions.

—Deuteronomy 32:10–11 NIV

The headlines in the newspaper screamed, "Miss America Mugged at State Capitol."

Governor Frank Keating had appointed me the Cabinet Secretary of Tourism, and I had to appear before an Oklahoma Senate Committee for confirmation. I didn't realize what was waiting for me. Legislators were at odds with the Governor and didn't like the idea of a former

Miss America handling the job. Their attack came swiftly and was brutal.

Standing before these interrogators in a cold room, I knew I didn't have enough information under my belt. I was a quick study, but the learning curve for this job was steep and many lawmakers were anxious to spotlight my lack of political know-how.

As I stood before them with a fake smile of confidence supported by shaking knees, I wondered why I was opening myself up to this. I had already retired from two successful careers. Why didn't I simply fade into the sunset and do volunteer work that wouldn't offend anyone? Why jump into this political mess?

Why?

Because risk is a part of growth and obedience. When God calls us to do something, He expects us to walk out on the end of the branch and stand there even when it bends.

Risk is going forward when we have nothing but the promise of God's blessing for the effort.

It is enough.

As author Brennan Manning writes in his book, *Ruthless Trust:* "The most urgent need in your life is to trust what you have received."

In time, I grew into that political job in spite of those who fought me every step of the way. It was a different game and God supplied all that was needed for me to play and, in some situations, win. The real victory was in my learned obedience to God's call.

— PRAYER —

Thank You, God, for the chance to grow our faith. Give us courage to risk, thick skin to avoid being offended, and a laser-like sense of purpose. Amen.

THOUGHT FOR TODAY

Risk is how we grow faith and live dreams.

ACCEPTANCE WITHOUT SURRENDER

I have learned to be content whatever the circumstances.

—Philippians 4:11 NIV

"It'll be okay," Mother would say when we faced difficulties. It was the grown-up version of kissing a boo-boo and making it well. She didn't just say that little phrase of optimism; she lived it.

As the years went by, life took its toll. Many of Mother's dearest friends and relatives came to the end of their lives and passed away. Her own endurance started wearing down. Then the stroke hit, robbing her of the ability to accomplish what her determination demanded. Life came to a screeching halt. She could no longer care for herself as she expected. The only parts of her body that still worked were her right hand and a sharp mind with a loving heart. How would she ever face a life with such loss?

When Easter 2005 arrived, I went out to the mailbox and found a card. Mother had sent a greeting card, which was no small effort for her. On the back of the card, with her weakened hand, she had scribbled, "It's taken a long time, but I've finally learned what the Apostle Paul said was true. Whatever the circumstances, I have learned to be content."

Mother taught me in many ways how God can take the toughest task and make it okay. Contentment is something we have to learn; it isn't a part of our nature. The first step is gratitude for blessings in life, even when they're buried and hard to find. Mother is thankful for hummingbirds, loving nurses, caretakers, a friend's visit, and church. If you give her a call, you likely will receive a thank-you note if she can write it that day. She feels blessed by so many things, and in turn, she is a blessing for all who know her.

That kind of peace isn't about circumstances or even happiness but rather acceptance and belief that all things can work for good for those who love God and are called according to His purpose.

— PRAYER —

Lord, there is a time to struggle and strive, but there is also a time to accept and acknowledge change. Help us to know the difference. Grace us with peace to handle tough circumstances without surrendering an ounce of hope. Give us contentment that grows from being plugged into a power beyond ourselves so that we may fly above the muck of things. Amen.

THOUGHT FOR TODAY

Acceptance is walking through life's unacceptable circumstances.

TIMELY PARTICIPATION

For we are God's workmanship, created in Christ Jesus to do good works, which God prepared in advance for us to do.

—Ephesians 2:10 NIV

As we look back on events in our life, most of us can remember one (or more) defining event, moments, something we saw or heard, that had a profound impact on who we are.

Mine came at a luncheon I was attending about thirty years ago. I don't remember where or what the event even was, but what I do remember was the person seated next to me. She was a Catholic nun, and in the course of our table conservation, she made a statement that has absolutely guided my life ever since.

"Service is the price we pay for the space we occupy."

At the time, my husband, George, was Lieutenant Governor. He would later become Governor. I wanted very much not to be just "the wife of—." We all want our own identity and to have the feeling of accomplishment. A series of events led me to become involved with the developmentally disabled of Oklahoma. I felt they were a forgotten group of people that needed attention and a spokesperson; they needed me.

With help from many people, group homes were established across the state along with workshops that made it possible for hundreds of these people to have the life God intended for them.

Through the years, these wonderful people have been my passion, my service for the space I occupy. They have brought so much to my life— their love for everyone and for life—no matter their situation or physical condition.

Teresa Bloomingdale wrote the book, *Life Is What Happens When You're Making Other Plans.* I really didn't have other plans, but the circumstances I found myself in as a politician's wife gave me the goal of finding a place, a purpose, and a mission to fulfill. I wanted to *stand up in the place the Lord had put me.*

Later in my life, on a beautiful day, while planning a trip with a friend, my husband came home and broke the news to me—he had just found our son, in his apartment—dead. The following days, weeks, and months, I hardly remember. My grief consumed me. I was in a deep, dark hole and saw no way out. I knew God was with me, loved me, and grieved with me. My prayer was to find a way out of my grief.

I knew being with others was "good medicine." I began remembering, as the scripture Ephesians 2:10 said, that we are "created in Jesus Christ to do good work, which God prepared in advance for us to do." My special friends still needed me, but more than that, *I needed them.* Their unconditional love has taught me much— patience, tolerance, and how to enjoy every day that the Lord has given us.

— PRAYER —

Heavenly Father, may I be ready at all times to accept Your forgiving love and to hear Your call to serve You. Amen.

THOUGHT FOR TODAY

It is in giving that we receive.

Donna Nigh is the former First Lady of Oklahoma. She has been recognized in many ways for her service to the mentally and physically disabled. Donna and her husband, George, have been servant/leaders in their church, community, and state. Among Donna's many honors is her induction into the Oklahoma Hall of Fame.

Prudy Gorrell

A SURPRISING FRIEND

Where you go I will go, and where you stay I will stay. Your people will be my people and your God my God.

—Ruth 1:16 NIV

All friendships are precious. But when a friendship comes from a surprising source it is a special gift. Ruth speaks the words above to her mother-in-law. It seems surprising in our world where so many families are hurting to see such tender words exchanged between a daughter-in-law and a mother-in-law.

I understand just how Ruth felt about her mother-in-law, Naomi.

When I married my husband, I realized that Nora, my mother-in-law, and I were very different—at least on the surface. Nora was a farm girl and the youngest of thirteen. I grew up in the city and am the oldest of two daughters. Nora, a former Army pilot, could fix anything. She helped her son (my future husband) rebuild cars. I have trouble changing light bulbs. I went to college and graduate school. Nora never finished high school. Nora married once and was widowed early in life. I was divorced, raising two young daughters.

Yet from the beginning we were friends! She was a single mom just like me. She understood my life. We both loved to laugh. We both cherished each day as a gift from God. Nora loved me fiercely and adored my daughters. When it came to life, raising my children, or finding my faith, Nora was my trusted ally.

When Nora became gravely ill, I didn't hesitate to suggest she move in with us. My friends didn't understand. "That's what nursing homes are for!" they whispered. I wanted this time with Nora.

We spent our days reading, talking about family, or just sitting quietly together. There were also doctor's visits, painful treatments, and scary nighttime trips to the emergency room. On Christmas day, she fell and we spent our day in the doctor's office. We both knew from that moment on the end was coming.

Still, the following days were not sad at all. How can you be sad when you are spending time with a devoted friend? Just like Naomi and Ruth, we shared a faith in God.

And then one day I realized what had happened—Nora had guided me out of the brokenness of my past and taught me I had a future filled with hope. It was a journey for which I had longed to have a guide, without even knowing it.

It was a gift from a surprising friend.

— PRAYER —

Thank You, God, for the gift of a surprising friend. Amen.

THOUGHT FOR TODAY

To have a friend you have to be a friend.

Prudy Gorrell was the owner of a retail gift store and then three MotoPhoto stores. She is married to the senior minister at Church of the Servant in Oklahoma City. She is Sunday School teacher to young couples class and active in every aspect of her church as well as many civic organizations.

Marcy Gardenhire

LIVING IN LIMINAL SPACE

My grace is enough; it's all you need. My strength comes into its own in your weakness.
—2 Corinthians 12:9 MSG

Liminal space refers to the state of living in between times of unknowing and uncertainty. Liminal literally means "to the threshold." I was forcefully pushed "to the threshold" with a diagnosis of lung cancer in 2005. Since then my husband and I live daily with uncertainty about the future, about tomorrow.

After three different chemo drugs, alternative treatments in Mexico, dramatic dietary changes, and eating asparagus four times a day, the cancer continues to outsmart whatever I throw its way. The emotional roller coaster we have ridden the past five years has surely taken its toll. Each treatment offers hope, but that hope quickly turns to another treatment failure and sends us to the dark valley of despair. Each valley is a bit darker and deeper and more difficult to overcome. The uncertainty of liminal space saps my energy and invites me to live with fear instead of hope.

It's as if I stand in a rushing stream, perched on one stepping-stone. There is no way forward. I stand in the present moment. Fear of the unknown, the rising water of uncertainty, is a constant companion. I wait for God. When my heart calms, God is there beside me, silently placing the next stone in front of me. The "next stone" has been a loving elderly lady who prayed for me in the grocery store aisle, a wonderful "Mom and the boys weekend" in Memphis orchestrated by my remarkable sons, a big "I love you, Nanny!" from my adorable granddaughters—stepping stones that lead me forward with assurance that all I need will be provided.

Living in liminal space has deepened my faith to know that God will always bring one more stone—just one—and guide me forward to one next step. The stones behind me disappear. As I surrender control of my life, my trust in God grows. God is reconstructing my kingdom to show me the way to discover His.

— PRAYER —

Beloved, draw us close to the warmth of Your grace when the cold of uncertainty attempts to paralyze us with fear. Illumine the eyes of our hearts to recognize Your presence in the small blessings of each day. Amen.

THOUGHT FOR TODAY

Live in this moment.

Marcy Gardenhire took the final step of life on earth at sunrise on June 28, 2010. She was a devoted wife, mother, and grandmother who left a legacy of courage and strength. In her final years, she was committed to finding ways to give lung cancer in women a more public voice. Marcy participated in five mission trips to South Africa where she supported agencies who care for HIV infected children. Writer Margaret Silf inspired the image of stepping-stones in Marcy's devotional.

Jane Jayroe

TRUSTING THE SUN/SON

We live by faith, not by sight.
—2 Corinthians 5:7 NIV

Only the prospect of seeing grandchildren could lure me from a warm bed at 4:15 in the morning. The day that greeted me was still dark and wet as an overnight rain continued to soak the Oklahoma soil. My car sloshed its way to the airport for an early morning flight to Newark, New Jersey. Drenched in the parking lot while lugging my bag to the terminal, I was finally checked in and standing in the security line. As I approached the gatekeepers, I dug for my driver's license, and dug again to the bottom of my purse, and then, panicked. In changing billfolds, I had left my official ID at home. After offering up most of my belongings, including lots of credit cards and other identifying papers, I was passed through.

At last, already exhausted, I sat squashed in the small regional jet. Lifting the window blind, I glanced with some apprehension at the sheets of water continuing to fall from the sky. As our plane took off, raindrops rolled across the wings like crystal marbles. The runway lights were pinpoints in the gloom. Faster and faster into the wet wall the plane traveled, gathering speed to lift into the heavy air.

As we flew from the earth, the airport fell away. For a brief moment, I glimpsed the city just waking up with a few blinks of light as if sleepy eyes were trying to open.

Then it was lost. We were in solid white space. It was as if we had flown into a bag of fog and were stuck there. No vision, no sense of movement. I felt anxiety heighten. Muscles in my face started to twitch from concern.

After about fifteen minutes that seemed longer than an hour, the dark white began to lighten and in a spectacular second, we broke out and skimmed the clouds. My inner exuberance reigned as we smoothly ran on top of a highway of cotton. The sun shone like a giant flashlight on the horizon.

I offered up a prayer of thanksgiving for the sun that is so predictably present. It warms the earth and brightens our days.

The experience took me back to a moment after my divorce. I was riding with my friend Sue, who several years before, had gone through a devastating marital break up. Sue turned to me and said, "It's hard to believe now, but I promise that some day you'll look up, and the pain will be gone."

I couldn't imagine a return to life without hurting, but in time I learned that she was right. By the grace of God, I worked through the clouds of emotional pain. Some days I thought the fog would never lift.

But the Son was still there. Jesus cried my tears with me, walked my walk, and quietly assured me, through friends like Sue, that I would break through and find another bright day. Like the sun on an overcast day, He was with me even when I couldn't clearly sense Him.

That's what faith is. It is being *sure* that regardless of what we can see, God is present.

— PRAYER —

Lord, You have brought us through many days thick with despair and confusion. Bless the beauty of our breakthroughs. Plant them in our memories to remind us of Your place in all circumstances. You are the True Light that never dims. Amen.

THOUGHT FOR TODAY

Trust the sun/Son to always shine.

Jane Jayroe

WORK IN PROGRESS

He who began a good work in you will carry it on to completion until the day of Christ Jesus.
—Philippians 1:6 NIV

"Are you the old Miss America?" the grocery store clerk asked in the parking lot. The woman had followed me out to the car because there had been a discussion among the employees as to my identity.

"Yes," I answered with a smile. Inside, I was aghast. How dare she call me "old?" Hadn't she heard that sixty was the new forty?

I wasn't embarrassed about my age, but I *was* concerned about feeling out of the mix, unimportant. *Retired* sounded like I was finished.

The Lord reminded me in scripture that He had not completed His plan for me—I was a work in progress until the end. Sure, I had pretty much finished several careers and raising my son, but I wasn't done with being useful.

God was calling me into new beginnings and the only one not convinced that they were important was me. The trappings of success might be different, but new roles ahead of me could be pregnant with meaning if I understood them as calling: a new ministry for women, a role as grandmother, leadership in volunteer groups, and the time to follow my dream of being a writer.

Clearly, God had plenty of plans if I trusted that He would complete the "good work" in me.

— PRAYER —

Lord, You knew me in my mother's womb and have loved me beyond measure ever since. Bless this new season and guide me into an ever-expanding purpose. Amen.

THOUGHT FOR TODAY

God is never finished with growing us up.

Judy Love

BLESSED
TO BE A BLESSING

> *From everyone who has been given much, much*
> *will be demanded; and from the one who has been*
> *entrusted with much, much more will be asked.*
> —Luke: 12:48 NIV

We opened our first filling station in 1964. My husband, Tom, had big dreams that began with this structure on a state highway in a rural area. I had a full life with two babies and a house to run. I wanted to be part of the action, so I kept the books for him and served in that role until

1975 when I returned to the university to finish my education.

We have always worked hard. In our first ten years of business, we expanded Love's Travel Stops and Country Stores to fifty gasoline units. We also grew at home with two additional babies. Today, Love's operates more than two hundred stores in more than thirty states. Our four children are grown and have blessed us with nine grandchildren.

Tom works with as much stamina and energy as he ever did and both of us give to volunteer efforts in our community. We understand that we have been blessed in order to be a blessing to others. Whether it's our seven thousand employees or our church, school, hospital, university, or neighbors, we give our best.

Working hard and giving to our community is how we were raised at home and in the church. It's how we've tried to raise our children. Giving is a part of who we are. We supported the charities and organizations that we valued, even when we had little. It's no different today; we simply give of our resources and ourselves. It blesses us.

When I was diagnosed with breast cancer many years ago, it was a true awakening. Now, my daughter is waging that battle. None of us is immune from tough times. But for those who *seek to be faithful,* adversity strengthens our resolve to live with purpose every day, contribute to the welfare of our community, and find joy in all circumstances.

— PRAYER —

Heavenly Father, we thank You for the many blessings and the privilege of helping others. Direct our every step as we seek to do Your will in the world. Amen.

THOUGHT FOR TODAY

Help us be joyfully generous.

Judy Love is Secretary of Love's Travel Stops and Country Stores and is President of the Love's Family Foundation. She serves on numerous boards including SSM Health Care, St. Anthony Foundation, Oklahoma

City University, Oklahoma City Museum of Art, Civic Center Music Hall, Allied Arts, Community Foundation, and University of Central Oklahoma Foundation.

Nancy Ellis

COURAGE

The Lord is my strength and my song.
—Exodus 15:2 NIV

"Trust and obey, for there's no other way, to be happy in Jesus but to trust and obey." The musical notes from that old hymn were soaking my sister's spirit as she lived those words out for all of us. The choir from her church was gathered in a circle around her bed, trying to give back to her just a smidgeon of the love she had showered on them, and so many others, through the years.

My sister was fourteen years older than I. She had been my best friend growing up; I even lived with her for a year when I was younger. She was as reliable as the sun coming up in the morning. She had been my rock. Now she lay dying from lymphoma, and our roles were reversed. It was my privilege and joy to be the big sister for her.

When we first received her diagnoses in the doctor's office, instead of panic or grief, a deep peace came over my sister. She seemed relieved to finally know what was wrong. Her faith was so strong, even cancer couldn't compete. She knew that God was with her, and she never faced the future with fear. In fact, now she had permission to stop struggling so hard to get better and to surrender to Him completely.

I said to her, "Well, Sister, you now know that it's okay to rest and nap and not try to work so hard." And she did.

She had always shared with her friends how God loved them and how important it was to trust Him. Now, she was demonstrating that daily.

When her strength began to diminish we visited with her doctor. "Medicine has done everything possible," he said. "You have about four or five weeks to live."

Family and friends gathered around as Sister rested in faith. It had not been an easy time for her physically. But spiritually, she continued to give to others. She had cooked and cared for people her whole life. Now her love was limited to precious and powerful prayers.

The night before her funeral I read the journals she had kept. They were full of prayers for people she knew. As a result, the next day after the service I could say to individuals, "She prayed for your recovery every day last month," and "My sister prayed for your son."

She prayed for others always—their jobs, their spouses, their health, and their spirit.

My sister blessed all who knew her, living with devout faith in Jesus Christ. She departed this earth, but she left us her heart. Her passing will always remind me of this well-known poem about death:

> *The death of people whom we love*
> *Brings sorrow and deep pain*
> *But if our loved ones know the Lord*
> *Our loss becomes their gain.*

— PRAYER —

May the peace of God and the freshness of the Holy Spirit rest in our thoughts and conquer all our fears. Amen.

THOUGHT FOR TODAY

There is freedom in trusting God with my life.

Nancy Payne Ellis is one of the founders of Heritage Trust Company, a lifetime trustee of the Payne Education Center, and a Deacon, Elder, and Trustee of the Westminster Presbyterian Church. She is a civic leader and a member of the Oklahoma Hall of Fame. Nancy is a devoted mother and wife who loves being grandmother to seventeen.

Brenda McDaniel

HELPING OTHERS IS A GIFT

The end of a matter is better than its beginning.
—Ecclesiastes 7:8 NIV

It was a Volunteers in Mission trip to Alabama that taught my husband, Tom, and me about the importance of being available for the work of God. We had come to help people who had lost their homes in a terrible tornado. The remnants of these houses sat deep in a holler, and the poverty was unimaginable as the people sought to find shelter in quickly built shacks.

Our team was to rebuild five homes while living in a local church. Tom's job was driving a truck to pick up supplies in a town about fifty miles away. One afternoon, I rode with Tom to collect what was needed to finish the home I was helping build. It was a beautiful autumn afternoon, and we were so happy as we witnessed the beautiful trees blazing of orange, red, and gold leaves. We started singing, "Stars Fell on Alabama."

We arrived at the huge lumberyard about twenty minutes before they were scheduled to close. As we walked up to the front entrance, an older man locked the glass door and turned the closed sign right in our faces. Then he just stood there, glaring at us.

Tom said to me, "Come on, honey, we'll get up early and come back tomorrow at eight o'clock."

I lost it! I started pounding on the door, begging the man to let us in because we desperately needed supplies. Without them, we wouldn't get our home rebuilt before we had to leave.

"Open this door!" I yelled.

Reluctantly, the man turned the key and let us in. He started asking questions about whom we were helping. Tom had shopped for supplies there many times before and is more patient than I have ever been, so he answered the questions.

Finally, the older man said, "You are helping my son. He is no good. We had a fallin' out, and I haven't seen him in years." Tears ran down his cheeks as he asked, "Why are you helping these people?"

"Our church believes that we are all called to help those who are in need," we explained. Something seemed to soften in him as we continued our discussion.

He asked for our list of needed supplies and filled the order. When we got ready to leave, he wouldn't let us pay. In fact, he insisted on filling our truck with gas. That evening, we were very somber on the way home to Glencoe.

The next day, we shared the story with the son, who was helping us. He stood still for the longest time. Then he said, "Tonight, I'm going to see my dad."

What a joyful time we had that evening in the basement of that Glencoe church as we broke bread together and praised God for this reunion. Tom and I had done nothing but let God work through us as an instrument of His love. As Mother Teresa once said, "We cannot all do great things but we can do small things with great love."

— PRAYER —

Thank You, heavenly Father, for giving us new beginnings every day that become wonderful endings. Amen.

THOUGHT FOR TODAY

God can use you for good this day.

Brenda McDaniel is the First Lady of Oklahoma City University. She has received many awards for her civic and church contributions. She has raised three sons and thousands of OCU students.

COPING WITH CANCER

The Lord is my strength and my shield; my heart trusts in Him, and I am helped.
—Psalm 28:7 NIV

My doctor's voice on the telephone put life on hold. I didn't want to hear another word. With my eyes closed, I received the message that transported me into the cancer camp.

I cowered in fear and begged God—not me!

My diagnosis was uterine cancer. The symptoms had been around for three months, but because of medical and personal mistakes, the disease had gone undetected.

I didn't want to tell anyone other than my husband—saying the word out loud made it too real. I'd rather curl up in a ball. Maybe like a bad dream the news of the dreaded disease would evaporate with the dawn.

All of life was in limbo now. Was this the beginning of my end? Or might this be merely a bump in the road? In this place of no sure future, faith was the only positive option.

I began making the necessary appointments. In medical waiting rooms, I picked up slick brochures full of information nobody wanted to learn. In 2009 over forty thousand women were diagnosed with uterine cancer, and 7,780 had died. Those numbers compared well against other cancers. They were still frightening.

After the big surgery, my support team of friends and family worked to double-check my medicine, make sure I ate, answer the phone, smile, touch, and pray.

Good news followed the lab report. Now it was just a matter of time, healing, and maintenance—or so I thought.

My recovery took a long time and was complicated by other issues. I learned: (1) The Christian faith is my core strength. It doesn't make life easy but provides resources for hope and meaning. (2) Physical exercise encourages healing. A couple of walking laps around the back yard in fuzzy house shoes are a good beginning. (3) Friends and family are forms of God's grace. A dinner left on the front porch by others is a multiple blessing. (4) It's important to *choose* to be grateful and happy! To combat the tough triplets of fear, worry, and depression, I armed myself with stories of survivors. I focused on what to be grateful for, each day. (5) Accepting death is a reminder to live fully. We all know that life ends and quality time is limited—but who believes that until we're facing it dead on?

I appreciate the lessons learned from this dreaded disease that robs so many people of so much. Because of my encounter, I have an increased appreciation for loving relationships, more devotion to the spiritual discipline of prayer and Bible study, and a stronger commitment to my church community. When tough times come, those human bonds and spiritual muscles will support the heavy load.

— PRAYER —

Healer of all, calm our fears of scary diseases. Give us courage to fight, wisdom to discern medical treatment, and peace to accept life as it comes. Grant us the grace to find gratitude in the midst of turmoil.

THOUGHT FOR TODAY

Trust in God.

Jane Jayroe

AN ENCOURAGING WORD

Be shepherds of God's flock that is under your care, serving as overseers—not because you must, but because you are willing, as God wants you to be; not greedy for money, but eager to serve; not lording it over those entrusted to you, but being examples to the flock.

—1 *Peter* 5:2-3 NIV

My friend, Kay Dudley, is small in stature but big in impact. She is kind and pleasant, the type of woman who raises great children and is a supportive wife, friend, church volunteer, and neighbor.

What you might not see at first glance is the incredible power this woman has dedicated to the kingdom of God through her encouragement of other people.

Kay's young adult life was spent as a nurse, then a stay-at-home mom and devoted wife. At the age some folks retire, Kay ran for political office and was elected to the state senate. After she served as a lawmaker, Governor Frank Keating chose her as his appointments secretary. This person aids the Governor in selecting people for the nearly 250 agencies, boards and commissions in state government. In this role, Kay influenced lives for decades to come by her ability to *prayerfully* choose people and inspire them to specific roles of influence.

Kay's impact went beyond state appointments. When Oklahoma City needed a new Mayor, Kay approached businessman Kirk Humphreys. He wasn't interested. Kay was persuasive and rather than accepting Kirk's "no," she asked him to at least pray about it over the weekend. In a ten-week time frame, Kirk ran for Mayor and won. He served two terms as a successful leader of Oklahoma City.

It was a long time dream of Wes Lane to be district attorney, but it often appeared a hill impossible to climb. When the opportunity finally arose, it was by the grace of God and Kay Dudley's involvement that Wes was first appointed to that post, later winning the election.

Dana Murphy ran for the statewide office of Corporation Commissioner and lost, but gained a new special friend—Kay Dudley. Kay became an ally for all seasons who encouraged and supported Dana when the possibility arose for her to run again. Against many odds, Dana became Corporation Commissioner for Oklahoma.

I had never considered being involved in politics. With Kay's help, I was appointed Cabinet Secretary of Tourism. I didn't know her at the time.

Kay was my mentor and encourager during the time that I headed up an agency of almost a thousand employees and a multi-million dollar budget. When I felt totally in over my head or was frustrated by the political process, I would talk to Kay. She would remind me that like Queen Esther in the Old Testament, I could have been created for "such a time as this." Years later,

I started a faith-building group for women in our city called "Esther Women." It has encouraged and strengthened God's touch on the lives of countless women through the years.

Who knows how many people Kay Dudley has influenced? She would discount all of her impact and point totally to God. But she was willing to be used by Him and be faithful to Him with her whole life.

All of us make a difference in the world. The question is, what kind of difference?

Can we be like Kay Dudley—in our families, in our communities, and churches? What difference would it make if we focused on people, prayed for them, and then fortified them in big and small ways? Could we be the encourager for someone to step up to the task divinely designed for them?

Kay would say to each of us: "Just offer yourself and trust God with the rest."

— PRAYER —

Thank You, Lord, for women like Kay Dudley and the many encouraging people You have put into our lives. Let us fill that role for others. With a smile, a word, written notes—maybe just our presence at a needed time—assign us to boldly uplift each other. Amen.

THOUGHT FOR TODAY

Let me encourage someone today.

Jane Jayroe has written this with the reluctant approval of Kay Dudley and the joyful participation of Kirk Humphreys, Wes Lane, and Dana Murphy.

Reverend Linda Brinkworth

REMEMBERING
A LOVING LIFE

Listen, I tell you a mystery ... We will all be changed—in a flash, in the twinkling of an eye.
—1 Corinthians 15:51–52 NIV

My son called to tell me a good friend of his was in the hospital, and he wondered if I could go by and visit. I was comfortable at hospitals. But this visit would be different. As my son talked a little longer, I learned that his friend had a brain injury, and it was very serious. This young man had been in my home from the time he was in elementary school. He had bounced around on the trampoline in the backyard and chattered at birthday parties and friendship meals. As I talked with his parents,

I learned that the doctors held out little hope for any recovery. We cried together, prayed together, and hoped together; but in a short amount of time the inevitable happened. Without ever regaining consciousness, this beloved son and friend peacefully died. Our grief was deep as we cried for the loss of one so young. He was only twenty-six years old. There were so many years ahead we would not witness, yet so many years completed that we would each cherish.

What could I say when his mother asked me to officiate a funeral for her son? I had to say yes, but inwardly I realized the difficulty of such a task.

Family and friends gathered to tell stories and create the service. I prayed and wrote and wrote and prayed. I realized that for my son and his friends this would be a very tender time. God spoke to me in the hours of preparation, nudging me to create a different form of funeral than I had ever preached before. Because I was familiar with this young man, I knew some of the things he would want his friends to hear—his pride of their accomplishments, his joy of their successes, his hope for their futures. At the service, I spoke directly to each of his friends with things I knew were personally important to one who no longer had a voice for us. I spoke in a similar way to his parents, his brother, and his sister-in-law.

I believed this is what was right and just and loving at a time of memorializing this precious life.

Since that time, I have heightened my commitment to live my life so that others know I care. I strive to treat others in my family and my friendship circles so that one day, when the breadth of my life is summarized, it can be said, "She lived a good life, loved deeply, cared tenderly, laughed often, and wanted the best for all of us."

I hope that as I awaken each morning, I can remind myself of this young man and the many others for whom I have had the privilege of preaching the celebration of life and live with a fullness that honors the life I have been given as a sheer gift of my Creator.

— PRAYER —

Loving God, give me the joy to share Your love as I live. Teach me to make this be the day that Your light shows through more brightly than yesterday and just a little less clearly than tomorrow. Amen.

THOUGHT FOR TODAY

Live today well.

Reverend Linda Brinkworth is an ordained United Methodist elder serving as Pastor of Care Ministry at St. Luke's United Methodist Church in Oklahoma City. Prior to entering into ministry, Linda served as a patient advocate in the Integris Health System. It was there she learned the critical value of each voice making a difference. In her ministry, this passion for the worth of the individual as a child of God guides each of her actions, especially when celebrating life at the time of a person's memorial or funeral service.

Dr. Lori Hansen

PLEASING GOD

Am I now trying to win the approval of men, or of God? Or am I trying to please men? If I were still trying to please men, I would not be a servant of Christ.

—Galatians 1:10 NIV

"What have you girls done to make Daddy mad?" Mother asked. "You must have done something. You both go and apologize!"

Of course, we had done nothing, but that did not absolve us of our responsibility for whatever it was that was causing Daddy to not speak to us.

My sister and I would hear that frequently when my dad would decide not to talk to the family for a day or two. No one knew why, but Mother thought it was my sister's and my responsibility along with hers to make and keep him happy. That, of course, was not possible for a man who battled with mood disorders and probably depression. We came to believe that we had the burden of our father's happiness, which for two little girls was quite a weight to bear.

It wasn't long before that translated into other relationships—family, friends, teachers—and I became quite talented at pleasing other people no matter what the cost to me. Determined young thing that I was, I found that if I worked hard enough I could just about please and make everybody happy. Of course, if someone wasn't happy with me, that could only be my fault. I just hadn't worked hard enough.

After I became a medical doctor, the circle of those whom I must please grew to include patients and staff. The nature of my practice involved a certain percentage of unhappy people seeking surgery thinking it would resolve their unhappiness. For years my sense of guilt and failure with some of these people grew immense as no matter what I did or tried, I could not make them happy. It never occurred to me that it was not my place in life to be the source of their happiness. I knew I could just work a little harder and that would make them content. I had made my success at creating their happiness a source of my own well-being.

Finally, it all came to a head when I had severe back problems due to several compressed discs. This was not an operable situation but only treatable with pain medications and therapy. God marvelously healed my back at a prayer service, but I discovered the pain medications helped to assuage the guilt I felt in not pleasing people and helped me have the energy to finish my day.

My body became addicted to the pills. Following intervention by my staff, I tried getting control of my situation. While in that process, I was called before the medical board for public hearings. It became a media circus.

Not only was I well known, but my husband was district attorney and recognized for his stance against anything immoral as well as illegal. My shame and humiliation cloaked me in darkness while I was forced to exist in the spotlight.

How could anyone who loved the Lord with all her heart be such a disappointment? I had always been able to control my circumstances—just work harder, pray more, and rely on my steel willpower. Now, nothing worked. The wall cracked, and I came tumbling down.

I felt stripped of everything: my identity as a successful doctor, my reputation, my position in the community, my livelihood, and my ability to help my husband's career.

I was so embarrassed I could hardly leave my home.

It took years of therapy, intense prayer, group counseling, steadfast friends, and a loving supportive husband; but God restored me. Can you believe that? What emerged from my shadow was a whole and happy person.

Along the way I learned important lessons:

- My heavenly Father loves me no matter how imperfect I am.

- I have only one person to please—God. What a relief that is. I please Him simply through my loving obedience.

- I am not responsible for the happiness of others. I can love them, but I cannot make them happy.

- I am the only one that controls my happiness, and I have finally found that there is great joy in the loving relationship with my heavenly Father.

— PRAYER —

Lord, You are my Light and my Salvation. We cannot hide where You cannot find us. We cannot fall so low that You cannot reach us. Thank you for Your mercy, grace, and completing love. Amen.

THOUGHT FOR TODAY

When my identity is in God, I can
live with what others think.

Dr. Lori Hansen is a facial plastic surgeon. She is married to Wes Lane, former Oklahoma District Attorney, and they share a passion for the Lord and service in His kingdom. Lori also enjoys photography, sewing, and her three doggies.

Karen Vinyard Waddell

WHY SHOULD I CARE FOR OTHERS?

But be ye doers of the word, and not hearers only, deceiving your own selves. For if any be a hearer of the word and not a doer, he is like unto a man beholding his natural face in a glass.

—James 1:22–23 KJV

She was blonde with curly hair to her shoulders, jeans, and a sweater set worn by so many teen girls. She was distinguished from the room full of "recovering" adolescents by the chubby-faced toddler strapped to her hip. He had her same hair color and olive skin tone, typical two-year-old drool down his chin, and his mother's beautiful curls all over his head.

I'll call her Sherri. She was fifteen, her son was eighteen months, and she had just completed over a year's confinement in a southern state's juvenile jail facility. She was sent there on a variety of charges, among them prostitution and theft, professions she had been taught since age nine by her cocaine-destroyed birth mother.

Today was a milestone reception for the teens—four months trouble-free. Sherri proudly showed me a note written by her classroom teacher that day. The note praised Sherri's progress and announced she had passed three school grade equivalents in the four short months she had been in school.

In those same four months, Sherri had been reunited almost daily with her son by the foster parents who cared for the child while Sherri was confined. The foster parents had no legal requirement to bring the boy to see his mother, but they did. During those visits to the lockdown facility—a two-hour drive from their home—the foster parents unintentionally fell in love with Sherri.

Their love was genuine. They announced they wanted to adopt Sherri. A love affair, that began when a modest-income family wanted to put their Christian principles to work, turned into so much more for so many, especially Sherri and her son.

Now the Christian couple in a small southern town, with two birth children of their own, have a third daughter and their first grandchild.

I tried to help Sherri's birth mother as well but she refused my offer of a home and of treatment. Sadly, after legally relinquishing all rights to Sherri, she returned to her life on the streets.

It has been four years since I met Sherri. She is a young woman now, with God leading her life, and she enjoys her beautiful son and caring parents.

God bless the foster family who cared. God bless the attorneys who managed the legal maze of adoption. God bless the social workers, the teacher, and the neighbors who now embrace Sherri and her son as one of God's treasured creations.

We can't all adopt or be foster parents, and few have time to get a law degree to fix the adoption laws. Yet I know there are so many ways that all of us—including me—can make a difference.

I must remember every day, as I leave my comfortable home and drive to my well-paying job, that there are hundreds and thousands of innocent victims in our world, both young and old. There are Sherri's all around me if I will seek those in need and remember God's purpose for me on this earth.

A pastor friend once told me, "We never make eye contact with *anyone* who does not already matter to the Father!" I can still close my eyes and see the pride in Sherri's face as she showed me that note from her teacher. For a little girl deprived of a normal childhood, her heinous past seemed erased. Her face reflected a beautiful spirit, one looking forward, not back, and one in the good hands of a Christian couple looking to make a difference.

— PRAYER —

Dear Lord, help me keep my priorities straight. I am here on Your earth as Your servant to use the talents You have given me for Your work. Help me remember that what I do or do not do for others makes a difference every day, caring always for all of the Sherri's of our world. Amen.

THOUGHT FOR TODAY

Help me see through Your eyes, Lord.

Karen Vinyard Waddell is immediate past chief executive officer and president of one of the nation's largest organizations caring for troubled kids, a former administrator of hospitals and foundations, and university instructor. She currently resides in Edmond, Oklahoma, working for the University of Oklahoma. She is also a motivational speaker and strategic business planner. Karen is the proud mother of two and grandmother of six.

LOVE OF SELF

> *Do you not know that your body is a temple of the Holy Spirit, who is in you, whom you have received from God? You are not your own; you were bought at a price. Therefore honor God with your body.*
>
> —I Corinthians 6:19–20 NIV

My friend Debra is a detective. She spends most days in a darkened room with a bright light staring back at her. She reads images of intricate lines and groupings. Too often, she will see a cluster of calcifications that will mean suffering and pain, possibly death, for a woman waiting in a nearby room. Debra's news will change the patient's life.

Debra Mitchell is a radiologist who specializes in breast cancer screening. The earlier she can find this disease, the better the outcome. Thanks to Debra's work, I had the earliest possible detection of breast cancer. With some minor surgery and follow up care, I have not had any sign of breast cancer in seven years.

The latest numbers relating to breast cancer indicate that about 192,370 new cases of invasive breast cancer will be diagnosed in women this year. About 40,170 will die. The encouraging news is that since 1990, there has been a significant decrease in breast cancer mortality, which amounts to nearly 30 percent.

We've come a long way in our ability to detect the disease early with good results, but there's still much to be done. According to Debra, one of the enemies of early detection is amazingly simple. Self-care: owning responsibility for our own health and accepting that our body deserves a best effort. That is not selfish or self-focused; it is smart. And it is practicing good stewardship of the amazing gift of health.

Every week, doctors see women who have put their health at risk because they are so busy caring for others. Regular screening saves lives. The Society of Breast Imaging and the American College of Radiology issued new mammogram guidelines in 2010 recommending that women begin routine screenings at age forty. We should all take this to heart, as well as pay attention to our body's need for proper nutrition, regular exercise, and rest. Routine screening for high blood pressure, high cholesterol, colon cancer, and addressing symptoms of disease can lead to a healthier life.

The Scripture tells us to love others, but it quickly adds—*as yourself.* We really can't serve people as effectively when we neglect our own needs. It follows the well-known directive of airline hostesses: "Put on your oxygen masks first, then help the person next to you." In other words, we can only help others when we've provided for our own life first.

I understand. My life always seems overcommitted. It takes time and effort to make doctor appointments and live according to their recommendations. Dr. Debra Mitchell is my hero for her lifestyle. For many years she has enjoyed a full time medical practice, volunteer roles, church activities, extended family responsibilities, raising three children, and being wife to a supportive husband. All of that, plus her passion for cooking and gardening, creates an efficient but often exhausted person. Debra has learned to care for herself in the midst of it all. She has learned to delegate, found a way to recharge through exercise and meditation, and understands that while taking care of many others medically, she cannot ignore her own needs.

All of us can experience God's love by respecting and caring for His creation. That includes ourselves.

— PRAYER —

Thank You for the gift of this body that works in a miraculous way. Give us the grace to be generous with care of ourselves even as we care for those we love and are called to serve. Amen.

THOUGHT FOR TODAY

God desires good health for me.

Jane Jayroe has written this devotional with permission from Dr. Debra Mitchell who is founder of Breast Imaging of Oklahoma.

Lisa Boone

YOU NEVER KNOW

Blessed are the merciful, for they will be shown mercy.

—Matthew 5:7 NIV

Our precious daughter, Jessica, was severely injured with a traumatic brain injury in a skiing accident. Her condition was critical for a long time, and the outlook for full physical healing has never been assured. Every step of survival is slow and painful.

Grief is a constant companion. It hits like a big wave in the ocean, turning us upside down and disorienting our world. But God is always there and is comforting our hurting hearts as we continue to forge this new life. Support from our friends and family is a blessing beyond belief.

Every day is a new chapter in learning to trust God's faithfulness and giving thanks for all He has done and the many blessings in our lives. We have learned so much.

One trip home from the hospital taught an important lesson. It seems like such a little thing, but considering what we'd been going through the past seven months, it was another layer of pain heaped upon our mountain of grief.

On a Sunday morning around ten o'clock, we were driving home from Children's Hospital following a major surgery to replace the first half of our daughter's skull. The traffic was light. We had to drive very slowly as I was holding Jessie's head and trying to help her keep from moving too much to avoid car sickness. There was a black car behind us—a Cadillac honking and honking, probably because we were going fifty mph instead of seventy. I turned around to see a very agitated woman, shaking her head and saying words to us. I looked at her and looked at her; she got more and more animated.

We were headed into a construction zone that forced the traffic to merge down to one lane, which slowed everyone down. The driver behind us sped up and zoomed around our car, leaving her trail of anger and frustration. She had no idea where we had been the last week, much less the last seven months; no idea the burden we were carrying on our shoulders nor the precious cargo in our car that we were trying to protect at all cost. My heart was sad, realizing she had no clue and then knowing how many times I have not had a clue when things didn't happen the way I thought they should. I prayed, "Father, forgive her for she knows not what she does—and forgive me for when I don't know what I do."

May we all go a little slower, listen a little more closely, and know that every person in this world has a pool of tears inside. Patience and love go a long way in this hurtful world. I pray that I never, never add to anyone's pain. Instead may I, somehow, some way, ease pain by showing love in all I do.

Blessed be the name of the Lord, amen and amen.

— PRAYER —

Thank You for every gift and blessing during this tough time. May we live out Your love in meaningful ways and always be mindful of the possible pain in the lives of others. Amen.

THOUGHT FOR TODAY

Help me show compassion for others.

Lisa Boone is a hospice nurse. She has been a leader in many church activities and is an inspiration to all who know her.

Lolly Anderson

LIVING IN THE PAST OF WANT OR THE FUTURE OF FEAR

There is no fear in love, but perfect love casts out fear.

—1 John 4:18 RSV

There were times in my past when I truly had to be concerned about my next paycheck and covering my expenses. Am I there now? Not at all. But sometimes I act as if I were. Sometimes I live in the past of want.

For example, just because there were times I couldn't afford to buy wine doesn't mean I have to drink a glass just because it's offered or available. Substitute eating expensive chocolate, buying clothes and objects, or any behavior (taking trips, going out to eat, fill in the blank) that has more to do with our past of want than what we need to be doing in the present. This thinking and these actions rob us of the present of realization.

Sometimes I live in the future of fear. I worry about losing my husband, Mike, to cancer, to an accident, basically to death. So I always want to celebrate when I am with Mike. It's the old "eat, drink, and be merry for tomorrow we may die" philosophy.

After all, my first love was killed when I was eighteen, my former marriages failed to last, and I know many who have lost the love of their life. My mother lost Daddy suddenly from a heart attack when he was sixty-six. Mike lost his first wife, Joanna, after forty-four years of marriage. Another friend lost her first husband and then her second husband on their honeymoon. It happens.

Fear makes me worry that my happiness won't last. If ever personifying Satan makes sense—it is anytime we let fear rule us. Fear is to Satan as Love is to God. Not trusting God is Satan's goal.

When we operate out of a place of trust, rather than fear, we allow miraculous results. (It's the third rule of the Universe in my book, *Magic Refrigerator.*) When we live in the future of fear, we rob ourselves of the present of realization.

Everything we have—each relationship with our loved ones and our loved things—are gifts from God. We do not own them; we are curators. Our duty is to show our gratitude through cherishing and sharing each moment we have with them.

When we live in the moment, in communication with God, our lives are filled with miracles. Eckert Tolle calls this the power of now. God calls this trusting in Him.

— PRAYER —

Dear God, today I will live in the present of realization, trusting completely in You. Today my fearful thoughts disappear as I let Your love fulfill Your plan for my life.

THOUGHT FOR TODAY

Help me trust in God for today.

Lolly Anderson is a motivational speaker and author. Her book, How My Magic Refrigerator Sent Me to Paris Free: 7 Rules to Make Dreams Come True, *was a 2007 MTV Movie Awards Celebrity Gift. For more information, watch Lolly's YouTube video:* http://www.youtube.com/watch?v=p1i17dK5jls.

Donna Lawrence

KEEP BELIEVING ... KEEP BELIEVING

And after the fire came a gentle whisper.
—1 Kings 19:12 NIV

I couldn't feel God's presence. Life was gray; I had no energy or enthusiasm, and getting through the day was an internal battle. On the outside, my life looked wonderful. Raising two children as a single mother was challenging, but my kids, ages eleven and fourteen, were thriving, and I loved my job.

The lethargy started Labor Day, 1999—I couldn't get myself out of bed. It felt as though a large truck had parked on top of me. The weight seemed unbearable and overwhelming. When I finally crawled out of bed, I felt weak. Day after day I felt worse; I found myself crying often, and I had no energy.

I pleaded for God to take this emotional state from me. No answer.

I asked Him to please help me feel better. No answer. I slipped into a deeper depression.

I was in a deep, dark hole, and as I desperately looked for the way out, I could see no daylight. None. I was in total darkness—in my heart, my mind, and my soul. I cried out every night, "God, *please* let me know You are here! Send me some sort of sign. Let me feel Your presence. Help me!"

Finally one night, while I sat totally still, stripped of everything I had always depended upon to make me strong, I heard a *very faint* voice. "Keep believing, Donna. Keep believing. Keep believing."

I clung tightly to those words. Night after night, I would hear the faint voice but only when I was still. So, I held onto the conviction that if I *kept believing*, I would be okay. It was God's voice, and He was still with me. My depression finally lifted, and I regained my strength.

We all have highs and lows in our lives when we can't feel God's presence or discern His will. Those are the times we often try to find our own answers. Psalm 46:10 says, "Be still, and know that I am God." How many times have we missed His message because we didn't *still our minds* and listen?

— PRAYER —

Heavenly Father, thank You for not giving up on us when we try to find our own answers instead of waiting and listening for Your message to us. Amen.

THOUGHT FOR TODAY

God wants to reveal His will to us but we have to be *listening* to hear Him.

Donna Lawrence is a certified executive and life coach who is committed to helping women achieve success—both personally and professionally. She holds a national accreditation in public relations and is a former nonprofit CEO. Donna is a frequent speaker for women's events, and she is one of the founders of the Oklahoma Women's Coalition.

Deliliah Bernard Hayes

THE GIFT

> *When I call to remembrance the genuine faith that is in you, which dwelt first in your grandmother Lois and your mother Eunice, and I am persuaded is in you also. Therefore I remind you to stir up the gift of God which is in you ...*
> —II Timothy 1:5–6 NKJV

The Bible is full of characters whose names are only mentioned once and whose stories often go untold. Two such people are identified in a letter from the Apostle Paul as he writes to Timothy, his adopted son in ministry. Paul writes about Lois and Eunice, the grandmother and mother of Timothy. There aren't a lot of details written about them, but anyone who was reared in a Christian home knows them very well. The reason most of us would know these women is because in reality they *are our mothers and grandmothers!* Even though their names may be different, the unmistakable truth is they represent the women who nurtured us and gave us the most precious gift we have—our Christian faith.

In my own life I can trace the roots of my faith to my grandmother Christine and my mother, Doris. I can recall how strong they were in the face of adversity and hardships. When my father suddenly died at the early age of forty-seven, it left my mother with the responsibility of rearing four children with limited income. My grandmother moved in to help with caring of the children while my mother returned to college. Doris completed her degree and became an elementary school teacher. Her faith in God gave her the strength and determination to survive in spite of the difficulties she faced. There were so many nights I would walk past their bedroom to discover the two of them on their knees praying that God would see them through. Their unshakable faith molded me and has helped me to become the woman I am today.

In 2003, I made the long painful journey home to attend the funeral services for my grandmother. Only this time, I was the one at my mother's side as she once again asked God to deliver her through this crisis.

Today, when I encounter the problems that so often invade my life, I remember the faith of my grandmother and mother. I think about how they overcame insurmountable odds because of their closeness to a God who loved them and cared for them. I often think about the gift they gave me, and when I find myself about to give up, I stir that precious gift, and I thank God for a grandmother and mother who gave it to me. I owe them so much!

Remember the Lois and Eunice in your life, and "stir up the gift" they gave you, for it represents the most precious thing you possess.

— PRAYER —

Thank You, God, for Christian homes and families. May we be the grandmothers and mothers who pass the gift to the generation following us. Amen.

THOUGHT FOR TODAY

Faith is the gift that keeps on giving.

Deliliah Bernard Hayes is the first lady of the Oklahoma Annual Conference of the United Methodist Church. She previously was a budget analyst for more than ten years with Verizon Wireless in Houston, Texas.

BONUS SECTION

Friends, I hope you have been blessed by the reading of these offerings for forty days. Spending time with God and focusing on scripture will grow abundance within your heart. Here are seven days of additional devotionals to encourage you in this new habit or the continuation of a discipline already in place.

If we ever doubt the importance of dedicated holy time, we only have to look at the spiritual disciplines practiced by Jesus. Whenever our Savior faced a crisis or decision, He withdrew from others in order to spend devoted time with God. As Os Guinness writes in *The Call:*

> *For Jesus, spirituality is plainly not a life of contemplation divorced from a life of action.*

There is only a rhythm of engagement and withdrawal, work and rest, dispensing and recharging, crowds and solitude, in the midst of one of the shortest, busiest public lives ever lived.

SMALL SUCCESSES

Whoever can be trusted with very little can also be trusted with much.

—Luke 16:10 NIV

"Why don't you girls sing while you do the dishes?" Mother said. My sister and I hated cleaning up the kitchen, and my mom's suggestion prompted our blue eyes to roll. Granted, we loved music, but Mother was tricking us again into making a small, unpleasant task enjoyable. "There's nothing I love more than to hear you girls harmonize," she said.

We filled the sink with sudsy water, cleaned the table, grabbed a dry towel, and got into the task. Reluctantly we began a tune—"Sentimental Journey," "Side by Side," and then favorite hymns. Before the final note, we had finished the dishes and our hearts were light.

Our parents worked hard at home and teaching school. We were taught that there was honor in honest effort, even little jobs. Enjoyment was optional.

Our dishwashing experience was a lesson in handling small things with the right attitude. Once we recognized that value, we were ready to push on to larger efforts.

Each of us has important jobs to do in life. We prepare for responsibility by dealing with that which is in front of us. Most of life happens in small moments.

God is constantly preparing us for significant work. We can approach every task with an attitude of our choosing. I can whine with the best, but when I consciously put God in the smallest detail of life, I choose meaning over menial. Joy can be a byproduct.

Like my mother, our heavenly Father is encouraging us in all circumstances if we are willing to hear His voice.

— PRAYER —

Lord, help us to discover extraordinary joy in ordinary moments. We trust You with our big picture, but never let us forget the small steps that get us there. Amen.

THOUGHT FOR TODAY

God teaches us big results in little details.

Jane Jayroe

WORRY WORSENS EVERYTHING

Do not be anxious about anything.
—Philippians 4:6 NIV

A woman at my church was the victim of a terrible accident. A few years ago, she was enjoying the hammock in her backyard. It was attached to two big oak trees that had stood their ground for many years.

All of a sudden, one of those trees actually broke and fell down on her head, splitting it wide open. Fortunately, she healed from that awful incident. But the cause of the fallen tree was surprising.

Little "carpenter ants" had eaten away the inside of that old oak and left it essentially hollow.

My friend couldn't see any outward evidence of that problem, but deep within, these insects had done a real number on the tree, weakening it so that the slightest pressure brought the giant tree down.

Worry works in the same way in our lives. We stress out instead of floating in faith. Anxiety does its work quietly and out of sight, but it's lethal stuff. Having our mind focused only on worry can take our life away from us—eventually destroying everything. After all, most of what we fret about never happens.

Don't let worry build a colony inside your body. What good has that ever accomplished? Not only are you not protected from difficulties, but an air of negativity and joylessness sits on your shoulders like a dark cloud.

This doesn't mean that we shouldn't think things through and plan for a positive outcome in life. We just don't freak out about every concern that comes our way and the many worries that we can anticipate in our imaginations.

Surrender your concerns. God deserves our total confidence. Fill your time with activities that build faith like prayer, Bible study, and worship. And don't worry!

— PRAYER —

Lord, it's so easy to fall into the pattern of anxiety—on the sad state of the world, a child we can't protect enough, a bad medical test result for a loved one. At times, the list seems endless, and the worries eat away at our lives. Grant us Your peace that is beyond understanding. Instead of wasting with worry, help us to trust and thrive. Amen.

THOUGHT FOR TODAY

Don't worry; be happy.

Jane Jayroe adapted this devotional, with permission, from a sermon preached by Dr. Norman Neaves at United Methodist Church of the Servant.

Linda Cavanaugh

CHOOSING MEMORIES

Do not conform any longer to the pattern of this world, but be transformed by the renewing of your mind.

—Romans 12:2 NIV

When we enter the room, the aura of its violent history seems to hang in the air. It's dank and musty. The space is dark, except for the light that comes through the door as we do, casting long shadows of our silhouettes against the far wall.

I'm standing with a man who has been here before—against his will.

Dan Glenn was a Navy pilot, shot down over Vietnam. The force of the explosion that ripped through his plane ignited the series of events that would lead him to the place where we now stand.

We are in Vietnam's infamous Hao Lo Prison. American prisoners of war held captive here nicknamed it the "Hanoi Hilton." It was notorious for the suffering and hardships the Americans were forced to endure.

We are in the room where Dan was tortured.

"All the movies tell you when the pain gets too great you pass out. You don't pass out," he tells me.

Our journey back to this place began months before when I called Dan with a request. I asked if he would be willing to return to Vietnam as part of a television documentary. Our focus was on the twentieth anniversary of the fall of Saigon, the day that marked the end of the Vietnam War. Dan's perspective as a former POW seemed crucial to understanding the war that had divided our nation.

He was hesitant to return, fearful the long-buried memories from his six years as a prisoner would surface. It was a time he preferred to leave in the past. But ultimately, he agreed.

As we stand now in the empty interrogation room, tears begin to well in his eyes.

I become concerned that revisiting this place so filled with misery and pain has been a terrible mistake.

I am wrong.

Instead of dwelling on the horrors that he and his fellow prisoners had suffered during their seemingly endless imprisonment, Dan is recalling the remarkable strength of the human spirit that allowed them to survive.

"I'm remembering the love we shared for each other," he says.

It was a love born in the most unimaginable moments of despair. Compassion fueled by a bond that grew in the confines of a prison ten thousand miles from home. An extraordinary feeling of fellowship that overshadowed the evil.

And from 2,265 days as a prisoner, that was what Dan Glenn chose to remember.

— PRAYER —

Lord, grant me the wisdom to know which of life's memories to leave behind as burdens and which to carry forward as blessings. Help me in my moments of desperation to see the bountiful gifts that You've provided. And, in Your mercy, allow me to experience the gift of love that shines brightly even in the darkest times. Amen.

THOUGHT FOR TODAY

God's resurrection love can
transform hurt memories.

Betty Catching

LEARNING LOVE
FROM LOSS

For where your treasure is, there your heart will be also.

—Matthew 6:21 NIV

Two days after Christmas, 1990, Bob had gone to pick up our grandchildren, ages nine and eleven, to bring them to our house. I didn't even see him when he dropped them off before heading to his real estate office. The children and I made a quick trip to the grocery store. We had just arrived home when my son-in-law rushed in calling loudly, "Something has happened to Bob."

We immediately rushed to the hospital ten minutes away. My husband had already been pronounced dead. I prayed over him, asking the Lord God to raise him from the dead. Finally my pastor, standing on the other side of his body, touched my hand and said, "Betty, let him go."

Bob had been found under his desk. He had been on the phone and said, "Something has come up. I'll have to call you back." Sudden death never gives one the chance to say good-bye. Besides being heartbroken, my life was suddenly different in every way. Bob, a retired USAF pilot, always made sure my car was clean and road-ready, the gas tank was full, my personal account was added to, and any household repair was fixed.

My forty-six years of marriage were not forty-six years of togetherness. I was always waiting months at a time for my husband to return—from India right after we were married, from China to meet our six-month old baby girl, from Vietnam after a year-long tour of duty.

I complained to my Lord, "God, I just don't understand." We were so dedicated, supporting the small struggling church we attended so faithfully. I counted on my fingers various deeds we should get credit for.

There was a great *silence*—like time had stopped. My crying ceased. I waited. I heard a voice say gently, *"I want you to love Me more than you loved Bob."* I was astounded. What was happening? "But, Lord, remember I did this, and this, and this..." Nothing but *silence*—then the same gentle voice—repeating the same words. Perplexed, I thought, *This is not coming from me and obviously not from Satan.* A third time I heard the voice, same words, and I knew.

— PRAYER —

Forgive me, Lord, for treasuring relationships, endeavors, and other things above You. Help me to order my priorities according to Your will. I want my treasure to lie in You, for there also will be my heart, as I am Your treasure as a child of God and live in Your heart. Thank You, Father God. Amen.

THOUGHT FOR TODAY

Love God with all your heart.

Betty Catching was a real estate broker for thirty years. She is a staunch Republican (having served as Social Secretary for Oklahoma Governor Dewey Bartlett) and a staunch lover of the Bible.

Jane Jayroe

THE JOY
OF FRIENDSHIP

Two are better off than one, because together they can work more effectively. If one of them falls down, the other can help him.
— Ecclesiastes 4:9-10 TEV

It was a magic moment. Hiking in the Saguaro National Park in Arizona, I watched the sun paint the sky in brilliant colors and breathed in air that a midnight rain had christened. As I started on the trail, my eyes were drawn to what looked like sparklers covering the mountain. It was magnificent—teddy bear cacti, covered with moisture in morning light.

Better yet, I was sharing the experience with some of my best buddies. They had come through thick and thin with me—my mother's stroke, my only child leaving home, singleness, a new marriage, my stressful job, rejection, heartache, and cancer scares—my girlfriends were always there. We had a lot in common through demanding jobs, dieting efforts, and relationship struggles. We were a group of women with serious responsibilities who loved to be totally frivolous in our time together, often laughing 'til our mascara was gone and our tummies hurt.

As we continued our hike in this special place, our guide explained the abundant plant life that thrived on what appeared to be a barren mountain. Our guide explained that desert plants often grow in a clump... a tall tree, a medium scrub, and a smaller cactus. They gathered in clusters in order to provide shade for each other, protecting them from the blistering sun. They didn't compete for food because their root systems grew at different levels. The tallest plant is even called the "mother" plant or "nurse" plant.

That's us! I thought. We friends didn't compete; we each recognized our own talents, resources, and circumstances. And yet our lives were supported from destructive winds of bad habits, protected from elements of heartache, and nurtured because we stood together. The soil was God's love, which deepened our relationships.

A planting of friends provides small comforts that feed the soul. In the midst of the big issues, small comforts are critical. Girlfriends hear little details, provide empathy, speak truth if you're dating a bum, always comment if your hair looks good, say you're not fat, and in general, love you as few others do. With the loss of our mothers, we girlfriends even begin to "mother" each other in both small and large ways.

Scientific studies indicate that women friends do more than help us live better; we live longer. The famed Nurses' Health Study from Harvard Medical School found that the more friends women had, the less likely they were to develop physical impairments as they aged, and the more likely they were to be leading a joyful life.

Friendships seldom happen in a hurry. They take dedicated time, energy, listening skills, loyalty, and unselfish love. There should be more to female bonds than current job situations, shared ages of children, or mutual interests of spouses. Details of life change, but healthy loving friendships are a core ingredient for joy. Don't expect a perfect friend, but try to be one. Invest in friendships for the long haul, and a great gift will be gained.

— PRAYER —

You have planted us in clusters for a reason, Lord. Call us to love everyone but give us strong affections for a few good friends. Thank You for the gift of laughter, love, and lessons we provide each other. Help us grow in Your grace throughout our histories. Amen.

THOUGHT FOR TODAY

Enjoy being a friend.

Jane Jayroe is blessed by many women friends including a mother, sister, cousins, nieces, a daughter-in-law, Facets friends, Esther Women, and spiritual sisters.

GETTING HELP IS HEALTHY

Because You are my help, I sing in the shadow of Your wings.

—Psalm 63:7 NIV

An accident at age forty brought a broken body. A divorce at age fifty meant a broken relationship. At fifty-six I was faced with a broken heart. My beloved husband died of cancer and grief overwhelmed me. Even though I had taught classes on grief management and established support groups for others, I didn't have a clue how grief *felt*.

I learned. It is slow and wearing and difficult.

I made efforts to get back into a life but it was an uphill challenge. I would make myself take the next step, get out of bed, go to work, go to lunch with a friend, and go visit my grandchildren. I just kept on keeping on, as they say, hanging on to a thread of hope that there would come a day when I would walk again into the light.

I clung to a note written by my daughter, Jayna. She had always been good at looking behind my brave façade and knowing when I was depressed or in pain.

On Easter Sunday morning, we were sitting in church, and in the middle of the sermon, Jayna leaned over and took an offering envelope from the back of the pew in front of us and began to write. She passed the note to me, and I read:

> *Jesus—sure He died for the downtrodden and the weary, for the poor in pocketbook and spirit, for the ugliness that this world brings, but He also died for the strong, who sometimes need to be not so tough and for the givers who sometimes need to receive.*

He also died for you, Mom. Being a strong person means handling the hurt, but it had never meant not feeling it.

This message reminded me during this time of grief that it was okay for me to feel not so tough, to receive when I didn't have much to give, and that experiencing my grief did not mean I wasn't a strong person.

In time, I discovered a strength and courage within me that would not allow me to give up. I began to understand if I stayed in the regret and the sorrow of what was no longer part of my life, then I would miss what was in my present moment. Eventually, I found a willingness to say good-bye to how life was, so that I could be free to embrace the blessed future that is mine today.

— PRAYER —

Thank You, Lord, for guiding us through the valley of death and despair. Comfort us as we acknowledge our own need and seek help. Remind us of the hope that is ours to claim. Amen.

THOUGHT FOR TODAY

It's okay to seek help.

Charlotte Lankard is a weekly columnist for The Oklahoman, *the state's largest newspaper. She is a licensed marriage and family therapist; founder of Calm Waters, support groups for grieving children; and former director of the James Hall Jr. Center for Mind, Body, and Spirit at Integris Health. She is author of* It's Called Life, *and a noted speaker.*

Jane Jayroe

FINDING HOME

Restore us to yourself, O Lord, that we may be restored.

—Lamentations 5:21 NRSV

On a trip to Alaska, one of the most impressive sights was the salmon fighting their way up river. I stood beside a small waterfall and marveled as the silver fish tried jumping the rapids. They were attempting to muscle their way up a rush of water that was like a fire hose. The Coho salmon were like shiny bullets being shot into the air, catching the reflection of the sun before they dove back into the turbulent white water. Their effort was admirable, their desire desperate—all for home.

We, too, are designed with that kind of yearning. Our goal is not a geographical place, but a spiritual center. God made us with a strong desire to find our home in Him. Until we do, we experience an emptiness that nothing fills. Material stuff, power, addictions, busyness, food, and all sorts of things can distract us, but nothing satisfies the crater in our center. Eventually, we recognize the feeling—inner homelessness.

Salmon are created to return to their stream of origin. There, they deposit their eggs, and their lives end. Already dying when their journey begins, the fish swim against the river current for weeks. Purpose-driven, they fight the water, the clawed hungry hands of bears, and other obstacles—risking everything to return home.

It's not until we struggle with our own river of challenges that we begin to find our way. Divorce, financial ruin, health concerns, unexpected changes, family worries, or emotional loss may force us to seek direction. When our emptiness grows deep, we wade into the water and begin the journey toward the Source.

When God calls us to Himself and we respond, we are rewarded by an overwhelming sense of peace, the power to go the distance, and increasing joy in the journey.

— PRAYER —

Lord of magnificent mountains, tall trees, and rushing water, remind us of the excitement of turning for home. Like a fish out of water we seek to belong somewhere—a space where we can safely sink into love and find meaning in our minutes. Amen.

THOUGHT FOR TODAY

Take a step toward the love and
acceptance of home.

Lolly Anderson, Lisa Boone, Reverend Linda Brinkworth,
Linda Cavanaugh, Betty Catching, Dr. Susan Chambers,
Coach Sherri Coale, Nancy Ellis, Marcy Gardenhire, Prudy
Gorrell, Barbara Green, Dr. Lori Hansen, Deliliah Bernard
Hayes, Justice Yvonne Kauger, First Lady Cathy Keating,
Charlotte Lankard, Donna Lawrence, Judy Love, Robin
Marsh, Brenda McDaniel, LaDonna Meinders, Dr. Debra
Mitchell, Kay Murcer, First Lady Donna Nigh, Bobbie Roe,
Jane Thompson, Karen Waddell. Not pictured: Kay Dudley